CELEBRATING GOD AND COUNTRY

by

Phyllis Hand

illustrated by **Elizabeth Nygaard**

Music by
Helen Kitchell Evans and Frances Mann Benson

Cover by Dan Grossmann

Shining Star Publications, Copyright © 1987
A Division of Good Apple, Inc.

ISBN No. 0-86653-390-7

Standardized Subject Code TA ac

Printing No. 987654321

Shining Star Publications
A Division of Good Apple, Inc.
Box 299
Carthage, IL 62321-0299

The purchase of this book entitles the buyer to reproduce student activity pages for classroom use only. Any other use requires written permission from Shining Star Publications.

All rights reserved. Printed in the United States of America.

Unless otherwise indicated, the King James version of the Bible was used in preparing the activities in this book.

TO THE TEACHER

"Let every soul be subject unto the higher powers. For there is no power but of God: the powers that be are ordained of God."   Romans 13:1

Celebrate God and Country is centered around "America, the Beautiful," by Katherine Lee Bates. "America, the Beautiful" was written in the summer of 1893 while the composer was on a visit to Pike's Peak. After she had endured a hard wagon ride to reach the peak, Katherine Bates surveyed the scene below her. She was overwhelmed by the majesty and grandeur of God's creation. While still on the peak, she composed the opening line. Later, the remaining words were written as she reminisced about her beloved country.

Children will learn the words to the song "America, the Beautiful" as they assemble the coloring activities found in this book. Pages 5, 15, 25, 33, 45, 63, 75, 89, 95, 111 and 123 contain the words of the song and appropriate pictures to be colored. Make enough copies of these pages so each member of your class has his own. Cut two pieces of white construction paper to 10" x 14" each. Have each child draw a picture representing our country on one sheet. Laminate both pieces. These will make the front and back covers for the patriotic book. Attach the covers by placing masking tape down the middle, both front and back. Fold six sheets of 12" x 18" white paper and sew the center of these into the center of the masking tape. Cover the masking tape and sewing threads on the outside cover with blue library tape. Use the first sheet for a title page. The remaining eleven pages can be used to display the coloring pictures. When the book is complete, the children will have a keepsake to remind them of the many new things they have learned about our country.

Celebrate God and Country contains recipes, choral readings, murals, crafts, songs and awards to stimulate the patriotic pride within each child. In addition, our religious heritage is explored. God has blessed our country in many ways. Our leaders have acknowledged their need of God's wisdom. These religious aspects have been highlighted through the pages of this book.

The culminating activity is a patriotic play. The costumes and staging have been designed simply for ease of presentation. On the day of the presentation, display as many of the murals, craft projects, creative writing papers, etc., as possible for parents to see. Enjoy learning about one nation under God!

DEDICATION

To Janice Bailey, who has been my team-teaching partner for fourteen years. She has the unique ability to bring out the best in each individual who is fortunate enough to be a part of her world.

TABLE OF CONTENTS

O Beautiful for Spacious Skies
    (Space Program)..................................5-14
For Amber Waves of Grain
    (The Land)..15-24
For Purple Mountain Majesties
    Above the Fruited Plain
    (Natural Wonders)..............................25-32
America! America! God Shed His Grace on Thee
    (Uniting Symbols)...............................33-44
And Crown Thy Good with Brotherhood
    From Sea to Shining Sea
    (America, the Melting Pot)....................45-62
O Beautiful for Pilgrim Feet Whose Stern
    Impassion'd Stress (Colonial Period).........63-74
A Thoroughfare for Freedom Beat Across the
    Wilderness (Westward Movement)............75-88
America! America! God Mend Thine Ev'ry
    Flaw, Confirm Thy Soul in Self-Control, Thy
    Liberty in Law
    (Our Country's Documents)..................89-94
O Beautiful for Heroes Prov'd in Liberating
    Strife, Who More Than Self Their Country
    Loved, and Mercy More Than Life
    (Heroes of Our Country)....................95-110
America! America! May God Thy Gold Refine
    (Presidents Who Led the Way)............111-122
Till All Success Be Nobleness, and Ev'ry Gain
    Divine (Our Fifty States Working as One
    Unit)..123-133
Play: Celebrate America......................134-144

SONGS

Our Rocket Ship..14
America's Beauty...24
Long Ago...32
God of Everyone..62
Pilgrims...74
A Part of History...88
Great Democracy...94
Great Americans..110
Our Presidents...122
States Make Up America................................133

Shining Star Publications, Copyright © 1987, A division of Good Apple, Inc.   SS843

America, the Beautiful

O beautiful for spacious skies,
For amber waves of grain,
For purple mountain majesties
Above the fruited plain.
America! America! God shed His grace on thee,
And crown thy good with brotherhood
From sea to shining sea.

O beautiful for pilgrim feet,
Whose stern impassion'd stress
A thoroughfare for freedom beat
Across the wilderness.
America! America! God mend thine ev'ry flaw,
Confirm thy soul in self-control,
Thy liberty in law.

O beautiful for heroes prov'd
In liberating strife,
Who more than self their country loved,
And mercy more than life.
America! America! May God thy gold refine
Till all success be nobleness,
And ev'ry gain divine.

O Beautiful for Spacious Skies

Bulletin Board Idea

O BEAUTIFUL FOR SPACIOUS SKIES

O, beautiful for spacious skies—those beautiful skies, those spacious skies offer a challenge to man. Once it was said that the sky was the limit. Now we have pierced those skies to expand our horizons and investigate more closely the universe which God has created for us. Americans loosened the ties that held them earthbound when they launched a spaceship carrying Alan B. Shepard on May 5, 1961. This astronaut made a fifteen-minute flight, but he did not go into orbit. John Glenn was the first American to go into orbit. He circled the earth three times on February 20, 1962. Each year since, man has added to his knowledge of space and has performed remarkable feats.

"... THE HEAVENS ARE THE WORK OF THY HANDS."
PSALM 102:25

Cover the board with light blue butcher paper. Make colorful planets and rockets. Write a date on a rocket which shows when a spaceship was near that planet or when a spaceship was able to take photographs of the planet. For example, on January 24, 1986, **Voyager 2** photographed the planet Uranus. The picture showed the planet's multicolored rings, and the craters and valley on its moon were also visible.

GOD MADE OUTER SPACE
LEARN BIBLE VERSES ABOUT THE CREATION OF THE HEAVENS

On the fourth day of creation, God made the lights in the firmament. The greater one was to rule the day and the lesser one was to rule the night. He also made the stars. Write phrases from Genesis 1:16-19 (RSV) on suns, moons and stars. Learn them in order. Mix them up and have the children put the phrases in the correct order. Place this game in a learning center for the children to review in their spare time.

And God made two great lights; the greater light to rule the day . . . .

. . . and the lesser light to rule the night:

He made the stars also.

FAMOUS WORDS FROM SPACE

On July 20, 1969, Neil Armstrong became the first man to place his foot on the moon. His famous words were heard all over the world, "One small step for man, one giant leap for mankind."

Compile a chart listing what each child would have said if he had been the first person on the moon.

OUR FAMOUS WORDS

"Who will follow in my footsteps?"

"These footprints will make an impression on the moon and at the same time make an impression on the earth."

_____
_____
_____
_____

LUNAR ECLIPSE SAVES COLUMBUS

God's universe is very orderly. Knowing about His heavenly calendar can be very useful. In 1504 Columbus had to stop on the island of Jamaica because his ships were no longer seaworthy. The Indians were unwilling to barter for food. Columbus and his men faced starvation. Columbus knew that a lunar eclipse would occur on February 29, 1504. On February 26 he called the Indians together. He told them that his God was going to punish them by making the moon disappear. The Indians just laughed at him. However, they were terrified when the lunar eclipse did occur as Columbus had predicted. They gave him all the food and provisions he needed.

Find out when the next solar or lunar eclipse will occur in your area.

MAKE A SPACE CALENDAR

Make a large calendar including dates from January through December. Try to write an event relating to space on each day of the year. For example, on December 18, 1958, the first radio broadcast was begun from a space satellite.

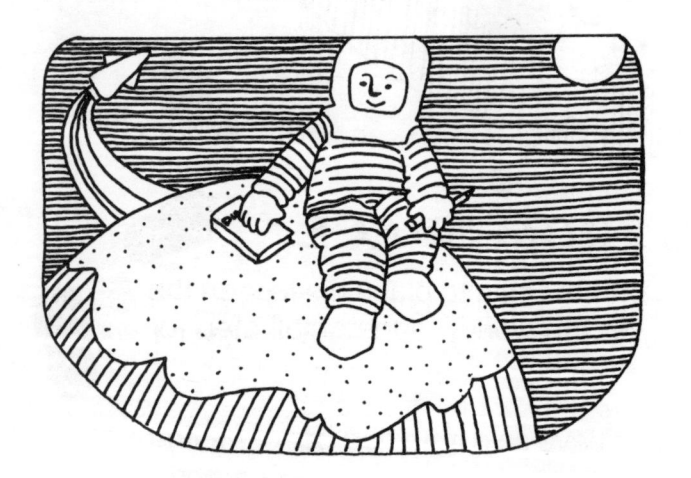

SPACE DIARY

Men have been left alone on desert islands after surviving shipwrecks. It is possible for man to be alone in space. Write entries in a diary detailing an individual's activities after he became separated from the other crew members.

INTERVIEW AN ORIGINAL SPACEMAN

Elijah was taken up in a chariot by God into the heavens. This must have been a very exciting adventure. Pretend that Elijah came back for a news conference. Compile a list of questions you would like to ask this original space traveller.

HAVING FUN IN SPACE

THE KINDERNAUTS

Looking at space through the eyes of a small child can often be an interesting experience. Have an older child interview kindergarten-age or younger children, asking them specific questions about space. For example: What is an astronaut? If you were an astronaut where would you go in space? What would you want to take with you? How long would you want to be gone? What would you do if you got homesick? Who would you want to take with you? Why would you want to take this person?

The older child should record the exact answers of the younger child. These could be compiled in a rocket-shaped booklet for the parents to enjoy. Entitle the book *The Kindernauts*.

SPACE SPORTS

It would be impossible to play baseball, football, or soccer in space following the rules we use on earth. Make up a new set of rules for playing the games in space. Do not forget the limitations placed on the game by the reduced amount of gravity in space.

DESIGN A SPACE TOY

Space children like to have fun also. Design some space toys you would want the first child in space to use. You might consider some magnetic toys. Remember, magnets would have more strength in space than on earth, as a result of the reduced force of gravity. Give instructions so the space child will know how to use your toy.

CLEAN OUT THE TOY BOX

Have children bring some of their smaller toys to school. Notice how they operate. Imagine the problems and complications the children would encounter if they were to play with these toys in space. Make a chart of the toys that could be played with easily in space and the toys that would be almost impossible to use in space.

MY OUTER-SPACE UTOPIA

From the beginning of time, men have wanted to build an ideal society, where peace and harmony would reign. Have the children imagine the perfect country they would rule in outer space. Assemble a set of laws to govern the country. Establish primary rules which cannot be broken.

SPACE CARTOONS

Create cartoons illustrating problems people encounter in space. A child eating his breakfast cereal and milk in the customary way would be impossible. Show what would happen.

Taking a nap would also present its own special difficulties. Show a child taking a space nap.

Writing a note to a friend would present unusual circumstances. Illustrate this common task in a space setting.

MOON EXPRESS

Make an application for a space flight. Include name, address, reason for wanting to travel in space, the scientific experiments the applicant would like to perform, and his health report.

MOON FLIGHT 484

Name _____

Address _____

Scientific Interests _____

_____

In 25 words or less, state the reasons you would like to travel in space.

_____
_____
_____
_____

Record details of your last physical examination.

_____
_____
_____
_____

How will the United States benefit if you are sent into space?

_____
_____
_____

WRITE AN ASTRONAUT SONG

The railroaders, miners, farmers, and sailors had work songs to sing as they labored all day long. Compose a theme song for the astronauts to sing as they blast off for their next venture in space. Use a familiar tune to help you get started. "I've Been Working on the Railroad" could be paraphrased easily.

I've been working on the spaceship

PERSONALITIES IN SPACE

Learn one or two facts about each of several astronauts. Write a fact on a rocket. Write the name of the astronaut who is related to this fact on a spaceman. Place the rockets and spacemen on the bulletin board. Have the children match the rockets to the correct astronauts.

MAKE A SPACE CHAIN

Starting with Goddard, make a chain of space events. Write the event on one link of the chain. Find an event which occurred shortly after this event. Loop the chain links together. Continue to add links as current space history is made.

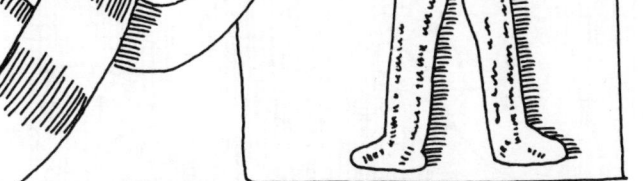

SPACE IN MY TIME

Draw an outline of each child's body by having him lie on the floor while another person pencils in the body shape. Starting with the feet, the child should write in events which have occurred in space since the time of his birth. The latest events should be written in the head portion of the body outline.

ROBERT GODDARD

March 16, 1926, ushered in the space age, when Robert Goddard launched his first liquid-fueled rocket in a field in Auburn, Massachusetts. Rockets fueled with gunpowder had been known for many years and were used primarily as weapons of war. Goddard's rocket used liquid fuel, a mixture of liquid oxygen and gasoline. The liquids were fed into the rocket from separate containers, and when they were mixed they provided power for the lift-off. Prior to this time he had developed the idea of using multistage rockets to go to the moon. However, the public thought that only a lunatic would consider this idea a possibility. To avoid ridicule, Goddard worked secretly on his experiments.

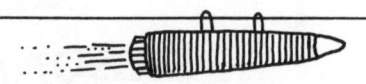

MAKE A CO_2 ROCKET

Purchase a CO_2 cartridge at a hobby store. Make a construction-paper rocket around the cartridge. Stretch a heavy cord from one end of the room to the other. Fasten the ends securely. Attach the little rocket to the string so it moves freely. With a sharp pointed tool make a pin-sized hole in the back of the cartridge. As the gas is released, the rocket will move forward rapidly across the room.

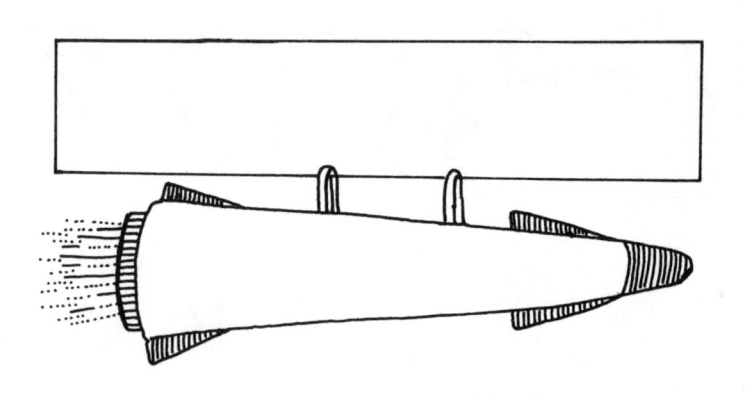

NEWTON'S LAW

"For every action there is an equal and opposite reaction." This is one of Newton's laws, which scientists use in space technology. Demonstrate this law in the classroom. One child should wear roller skates. Another child should be about ten feet away from the first child. The child with the roller skates should throw a heavy item, like a medicine ball, to the other child. As the child pushes forward to throw the ball, he rolls backward on the roller skates.

MAKE AN ASTRONAUT PUPPET

Each child will need a white paper bag, some narrow strips of red and blue construction paper, a piece of aluminum foil, and a sheet of white construction paper. Cut arms and legs from the white construction paper. Glue them to the paper bag, which serves as the puppet's body. Cut an aluminum-foil facepiece for the astronaut's helmet. Attach two blue eyes in the center of the facepiece. Glue this to the bottom of the bag. Use the narrow strips to decorate the astronaut's uniform.

WRITE AN ASTRONAUT PLAY

Imagine the conversation the astronauts might have concerning their feelings about their upcoming flights. Have the children work in pairs to write the conversation in play form. Allow the children to perform the play they have written, using the astronaut puppets.

OUR ROCKET SHIP

Words by Helen Kitchell Evans
Music by Frances Mann Benson

Let's all get in-to our space suit; the rock-et ship is now in place; A great blast will send us fast in-to the outer space, oh come now eve-ry one let's go A-round the earth we'll race; We'll look out-side and see the stars that God put in-to place; Oh, look be-low and see the earth, God's grass and trees be-low, He made the earth for us be-cause he loves us so.

Shining Star Publications, Copyright © 1987, A division of Good Apple, Inc.   SS843

For Amber Waves of Grain

SOW GOOD SEEDS

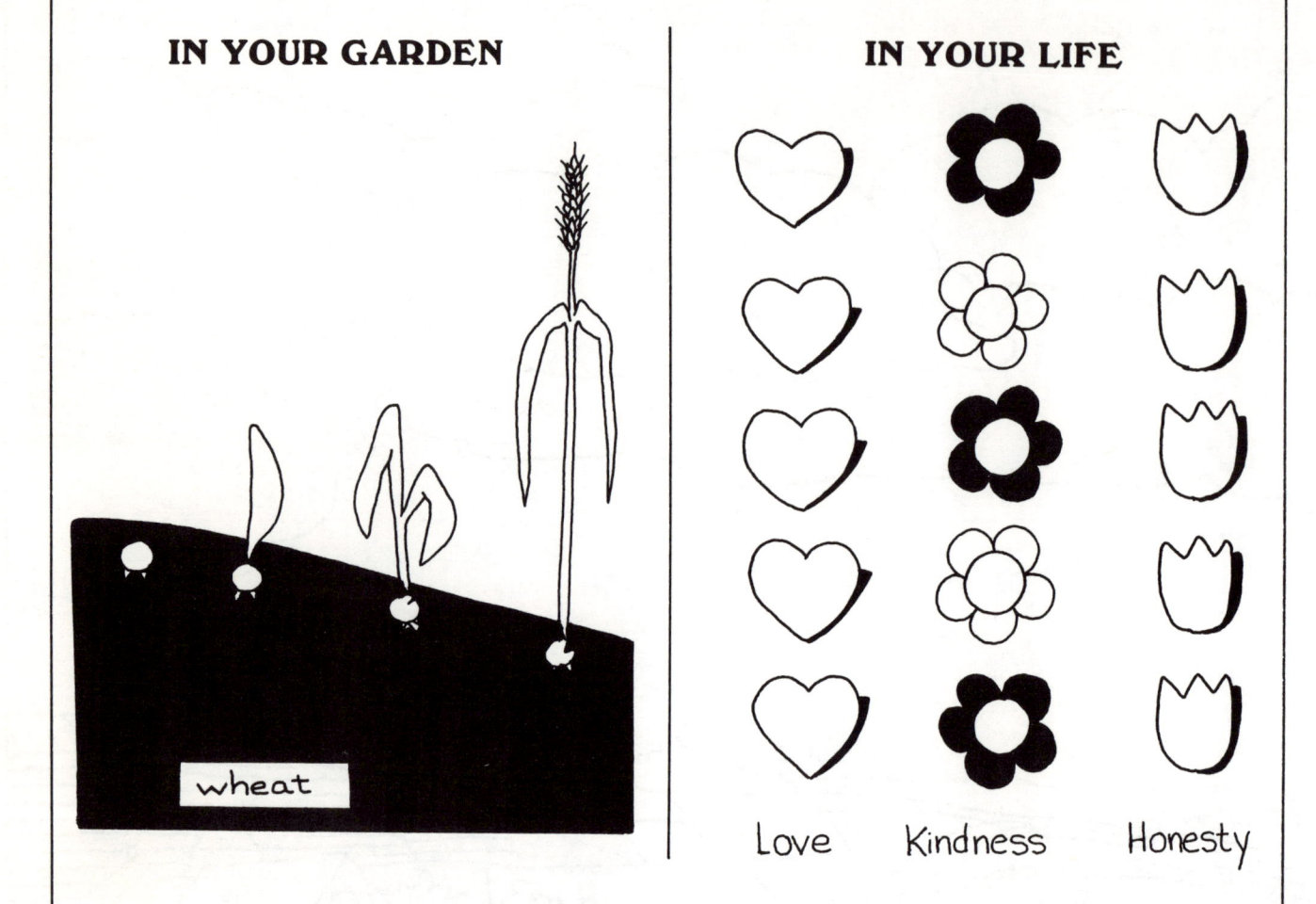

IN YOUR GARDEN

IN YOUR LIFE

Love   Kindness   Honesty

". . . whatsoever a man soweth, that shall he also reap."   Galatians 6:7

Cover the bulletin board with blue or yellow butcher paper. Use black letters. On each of the hearts and flowers, have the children write one example of a time they sowed good seeds in their garden of life.

Memorize Galatians 6:7. "Be not deceived; God is not mocked: for whatsoever a man soweth, that shall he also reap."

WHEAT—THE STAFF OF LIFE

People began to grow wheat many thousands of years ago. It is the grain from which most breads are made. It can be stored for long periods of time without spoiling. Wheat can be grown on low plains or in high mountain areas. It does not need a great amount of rainfall. There are two kinds of wheat, winter wheat and spring wheat. Winter wheat is planted in the fall and harvested in the summer. Spring wheat is planted in the spring and harvested in late summer. Most wheat is ground into flour for bread. Wheat is also used for spaghetti, macaroni, cereals, health foods, and livestock food.

HAVE A FOOD FAIR

Enlist the children to read labels on food products. Bring packaged foods to school that have wheat listed on the labels.

SPROUT WHEAT SEEDS

Growing wheat seeds is like having a year-round garden. By sprouting wheat and eating the sprouts, one can provide a high source of vitamins.

To sprout the wheat seeds, place about one-fourth cup seeds in a quart jar. Cover the seeds with warm water. Place a cheesecloth over the mouth of the jar. Secure it with a rubber band. Allow the seeds to soak overnight. In the morning drain the water and rinse the seeds. Drain off as much water as possible. Wrap the jar in a towel and lay it on its side. The sprouts will be more tender if they are sprouted in the dark. Rinse the seeds three times daily until they are ready to eat. Wheat sprouts should be eaten before the leaves appear. After this time they become tough. On the day you will eat the sprouts, remove the towel so that light can reach them.

THE WHEAT FESTIVAL

The wheat harvest was an important time in the lives of the ancients. The Jewish people observed the Feast of Weeks, in which they offered the first of the wheat harvest to God. This was a sacred occasion in which a shaft of wheat was waved back and forth to symbolize all of the wheat still in the fields. This festival was also called Pentecost. Bread was not to be made from the new grain until the first of the crop was offered to God. In this way the people thanked God for the harvest. The celebration took place seven weeks after Passover. On this day no one was to work. Instead, all inhabitants, even strangers, were to join in the happy celebration. After the festival, the women were free to use the grain for making bread.

Make whole wheat bread. If a wheat grinder is available, grind the wheat while the children watch. If a grinder is not available, regular whole wheat flour may be used.

FAVORITE WHOLE WHEAT BREAD

Dissolve the yeast in the water, add sugar and allow the mixture to rise.

4 tsp. granular yeast
1 cup warm water
1 tsp. sugar

Peel the potato and cook in water until tender. Mash the potato, and return the liquid to the potato. Pour the potato mixture and the yeast mixture into a large bowl.

1 quart water
1 medium potato

Add these ingredients to the above and mix thoroughly. Cover with a wet, warm cloth and allow to rise for an hour.

4 tsp. salt
3 tsp. sugar
3 cups freshly ground whole wheat flour

Melt margarine and mix into bread sponge. Add the flour and knead for about ten minutes. Cover and place in warm spot. Let rise until double in bulk. Punch down and let rise two more times.

½ cup margarine
2 cups whole wheat flour
7 cups white flour

Divide the dough into four equal pieces. Pound each section hard to release air bubbles. Shape into loaves and place two to a cookie sheet. Pierce the top of each one several times with a fork. Allow to rise until about double in bulk. Bake at 425° for 25 minutes. Yields four loaves.

BREAD FOR A MIRACLE

In biblical times two main types of bread were used. The rich people ate wheat bread, while the poorer class consumed barley bread. Jesus used a poor little boy's five barley loaves and two small fish to feed a crowd of 5,000 people. Tell this story from John 6:1-14. Have the children pretend to be the child who gave the lunch to Jesus on that day. Have them write a story about what they told their mother when they arrived home.

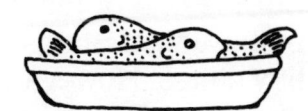

My Lunch

You'll never believe what happened to my lunch today!

I AM THE BREAD OF LIFE

Bread was the staple food in the lives of early people. It was hard to survive without it. Jesus used this idea to help the people realize they could not live without God either. Jesus said He was the Bread of Life. Help the children memorize John 6:47-51. Present the Bread of Life Award to those who learn the verses.

BREAD OF LIFE AWARD

This certifies that

_____

has learned John 6:47-51.

_____
date

_____
signature

CORN

Corn is one of the most valuable products of the United States. It is grown in all of the fifty states. However, most of it comes from the Corn Belt, which is located in the midwestern states. This area has deep, rich soil and long, hot summers to make the corn grow tall. Each American eats about fifty pounds of corn every year. There are dozens of ways corn can be used. Make a giant ear of corn and place it on the wall. Give each child a few kernels cut from yellow construction paper. Each time a child can name a corn recipe or name a use for corn, he may write this use on a kernel and place it on the corn. Some suggestions include corn chowder, popcorn, corn oil, syrup, gum, candy, cornflakes, hominy, succotash, feed for animals, and glue.

CORN IN THE BIBLE

The word **corn** is derived from a word that means "grain of any kind." Therefore, the corn mentioned in the Bible could have been wheat, barley, or any other cereal grain. It was the duty of the women to grind the corn. In early times they ground it between two rocks. Often the women would spend half a day grinding the grain fine enough to be used in their breads. It was considered disgraceful for a man to have to grind the corn. When an enemy took the Israelites as captives, they often made the men grind the corn. Samson had to do this while he was in prison. (Judges 16:21)

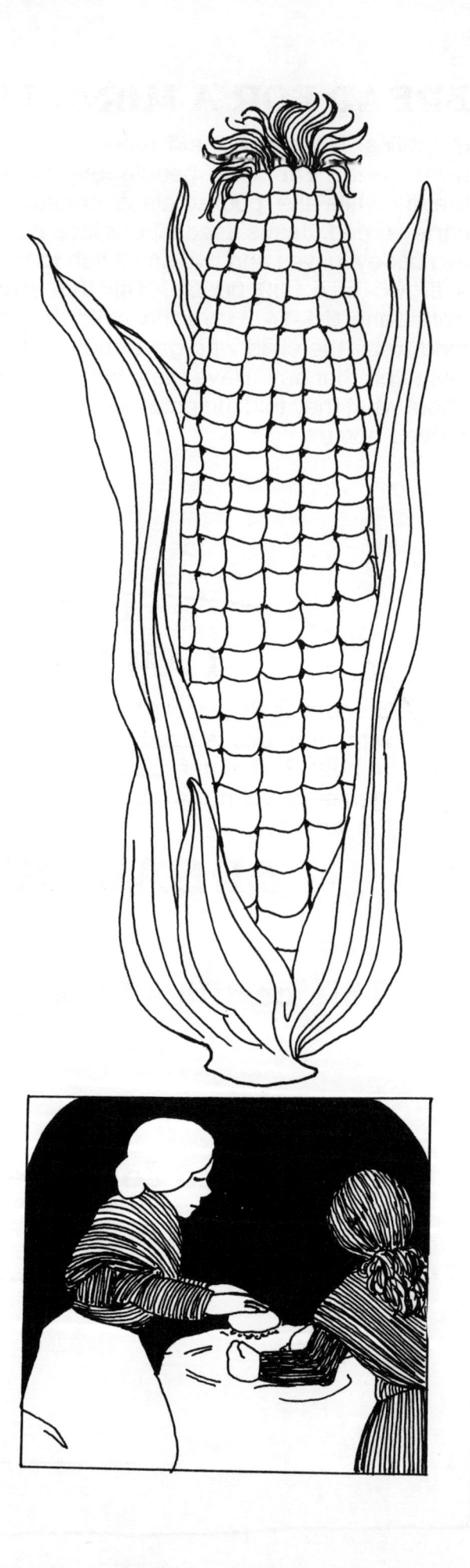

INDIAN CORN

Botanists believe that corn is truly an American vegetable. It was unknown in Europe at the time of Columbus' voyage in 1492.

Corn was very important to the American Indians. Their survival often depended on how great a supply of corn they possessed. Because of its importance, many of their religious ceremonies centered around corn. There was a ceremony to bless the seeds. Later, the young plants were blessed. Another religious ceremony was held at harvest time. This was the Indians' way of thanking God for providing for them.

Many varieties of corn were grown by the Indians. Using the various kinds, they devised a great many recipes for corn. The woodland Indians created succotash when they used beans with corn. Indians made use of cornmeal in making breads or cereals, and they enjoyed popcorn, which they cooked in special clay pots placed in the fire.

Have a popcorn party. Make a popcorn picture while you are eating the treat. Draw an outline of a simple object and fill it in with popcorn. To make special features such as eyes or mouth, color the popcorn with food dyes.

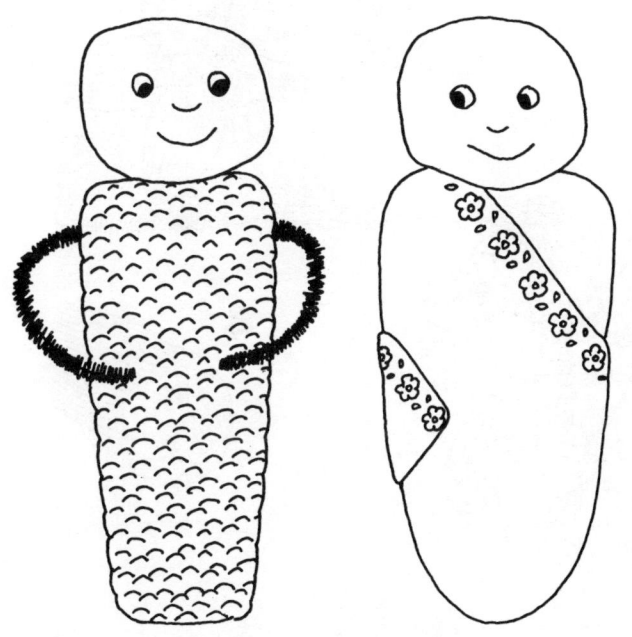

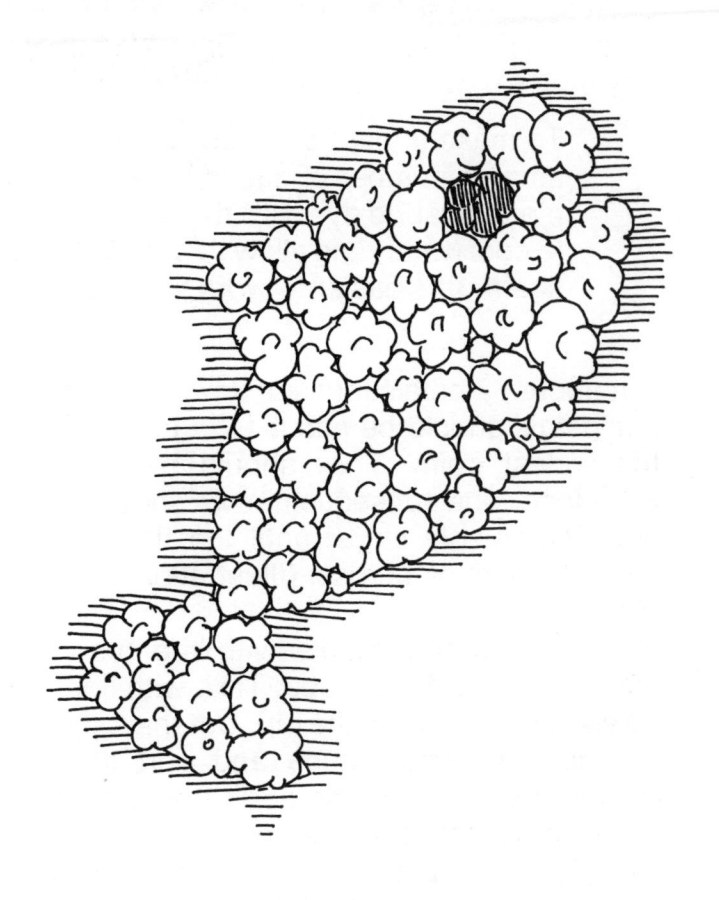

WASTE NOT WANT NOT

Pioneers used every part of the corn plant. The kernels were eaten by the family or their animals. The cobs were dried and used for fuel or making toys. The husks were dried and made into mats for the floor or brooms for sweeping the floor. The leaves from the stalk could be stuffed into ticking for mattresses. The corn stalk was eaten by the animals. Make a corncob doll:

Dry a corncob. Cut a one-inch section for the head. Attach the head to the body with the round surface forming the face. Glue in place and secure with straight pins. Use a felt pen to draw the face. Wrap an eight-inch square of flannel around the "baby."

MAKE A GIANT CORNHUSK SUNFLOWER

To make a giant cornhusk sunflower, first dye some cornhusks yellow and a smaller number of husks brown. Follow the directions on a package of commercial fabric dye. Stir the husks until they are the desired shade. Rinse them in cool water, and allow to dry. When you are ready to use them, wet the husks again. It is easier to work with damp husks.

Cut about 32 petals for each flower. The inner petals should be about 1½" across at the widest point. They should be about 2½" long. The subsequent rows should be cut increasingly larger until the flower is about six inches across. (Illustration 1.)

Beginning in the middle with the brown husks, make a 4-inch tube. Tie it with floral wire about 2½" from the top. Cut the top of the husk in small strips and curl them around a pencil, twisting and turning them to form a rounded center. Attach the smallest yellow petals to this center section by wrapping wire around the base of each one. Continue to add the larger petals until the flower is the desired size.
(Illustration 2.)

Wrap the base of the flower securely. Add heavier floral wire and cover with floral tape to make a stem. (Illustration 3.)

While the petals are still damp, shape them by curling the outer ends underneath.
(Illustration 4.)

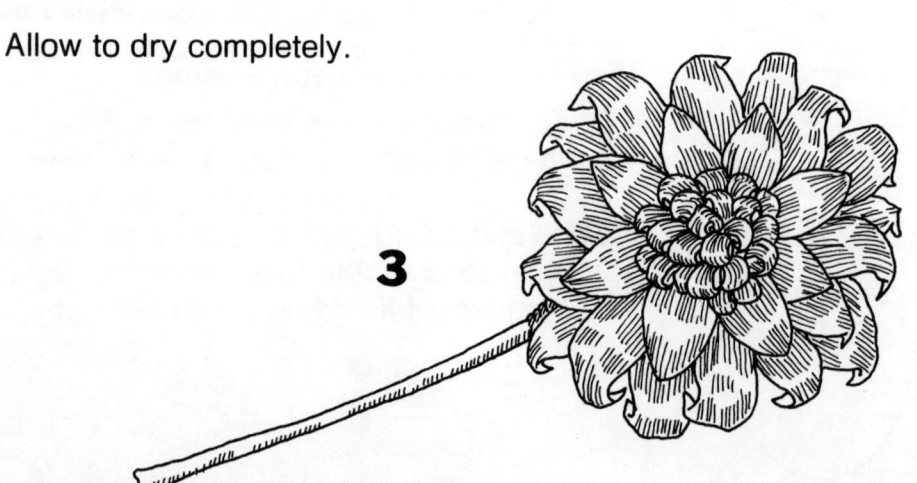

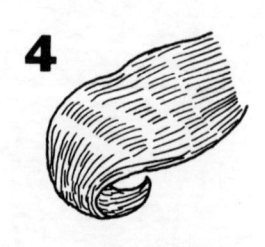

Allow to dry completely.

Shining Star Publications, Copyright © 1987, A division of Good Apple, Inc.

SS843

GLEANER GIRL

Ruth had to glean the fields in Naomi's homeland to provide a living for the two women. Tell the story from the book of Ruth.

MAKE A FLASH-CARD GAME
Make fifteen flash cards on yellow poster board. Write a question on the front of each card and place the answer on the back.

Two children may play this game. They should study the flash cards until they think they know all the answers. Then they may take turns flashing the cards to one another.

In what country was Ruth born?
Ruth 1:4

1. In what country was Ruth born? (Ruth 1:4)
2. Who were the first husbands of Orpah and Ruth? (Ruth 1:4,5)
3. What city was Naomi's home? (Ruth 1:19)
4. Which girl decided to go to Bethlehem with Naomi? (Ruth 1:14)
5. Which girl decided to stay in Moab? (Ruth 1:14)
6. What grain were the people harvesting when Ruth arrived in Bethlehem? (Ruth 2:2)
7. What is a person called who picks up grain left by the reapers? (Ruth 2:2)
8. Who owned the field where Ruth gleaned? (Ruth 2:3)
9. Who invited Ruth to have lunch with him? (Ruth 2:14)
10. What other kind of grain did Ruth glean besides barley? (Ruth 2:23)
11. Who said that Boaz could be their kinsman-redeemer? (Ruth 2:20)
12. Why did Boaz not redeem Naomi's property immediately? (Ruth 4:4)
13. Who married Boaz? (Ruth 4:13)
14. What was Ruth's son's name? (Ruth 4:17)
15. What famous king was a great-grandson of Ruth? (Ruth 4:22)

Moab	Corn (Barley)	Naomi
Mahlon and Chilion	A gleaner	There was a closer relative.
Bethlehem	Boaz	Ruth
Ruth	Boaz	Obed
Orpah	Wheat	David

AMERICA'S BEAUTY

Words by Helen Kitchell Evans
Music by Frances Mann Benson

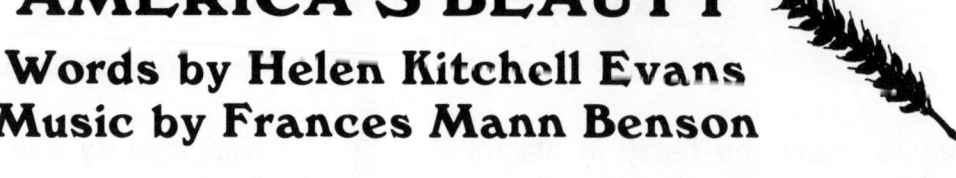

The hills and the val-leys, The fields filled with grain; I love my home, and I'm proud of her name. A-mer-i-ca's scen-ery is nev-er the same,— nev-er, no nev-er the same. Wheat-fields and corn-fields a-long each coun-try lane; May God's great coun-try re-main ev — er the same.

For Purple Mountain Majesties
Above the Fruited Plain

Bulletin Board Idea

SEVEN NATURAL WONDERS

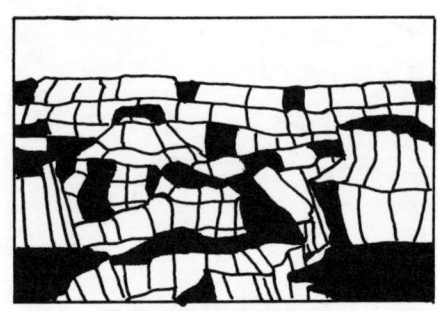

GRAND CANYON

REDWOOD TREES

YELLOWSTONE PARK

CARLSBAD CAVERNS

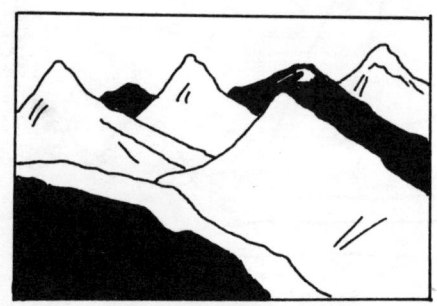

ROCKY MOUNTAINS

CRATER LAKE

MISSISSIPPI RIVER

"And God called the dry land Earth; and the gathering together of the waters he called Seas: and God saw that it was good." Genesis 1:10

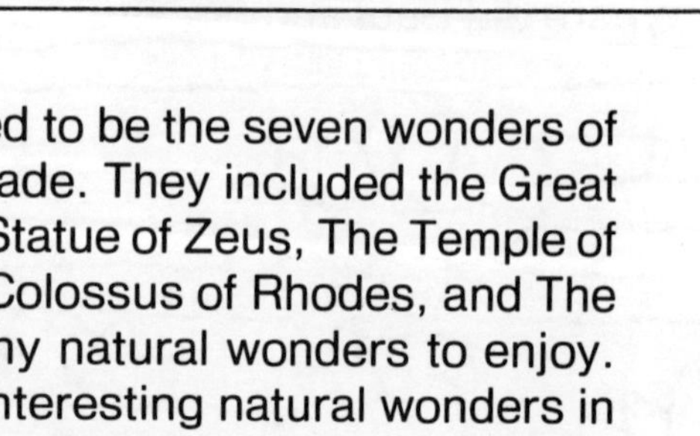

Ancient travelers listed structures they considered to be the seven wonders of the ancient world. Their wonders were all man-made. They included the Great Pyramid, The Hanging Gardens of Babylon, The Statue of Zeus, The Temple of Artemis, The Mausoleum at Halicarnassus, The Colossus of Rhodes, and The Lighthouse of Alexandria. God has given us many natural wonders to enjoy. By popular vote of the children, select the most interesting natural wonders in the United States. Have the children draw pictures of these seven wonders and display them on the bulletin board. (Pictures may also be cut from magazines.)

ROCKY MOUNTAIN NATIONAL PARK

Towering peaks provide breathtaking views of God's handiwork in the northern section of Colorado. Winter winds howl at more than two hundred miles per hour atop the ridges in Rocky Mountain National Park. Hardy plants sink their roots deep into the rocky crevasses to sustain life. Snow buttercups begin to dot the landscape even before the snow has melted. Little animals, such as pikas and marmots, feed on the vegetation.

BIBLICAL MOUNTAINS

Many important biblical events occurred on or near mountains. Make a flash-card game to help the children learn about the mountains. Make ten cards as shown. Write a question on the front of each card and the answer on the back. Two people may play this game. Have the players study the cards until they know them, and then take turns flashing the cards to one another.

Where did Joshua build an altar to the Lord? Joshua 8:30

MOUNTAIN GAME

1. Where did Jacob go when he ran away from Laban? (Genesis 31:21)
2. Where did Esau live? (Genesis 36:8)
3. Where was the Lord going to appear? (Exodus 19:11)
4. Where did the glory of the Lord abide? (Exodus 24:16)
5. Where did Aaron die? (Numbers 20:25)
6. Where did Joshua build an altar to the Lord? (Joshua 8:30)
7. Where did Deborah fight Sisera's army? (Judges 4:6)
8. Where did Saul and his three sons die? (I Samuel 31:8)
9. Where did Elijah challenge the prophets of Baal? (I Kings 18:20)
10. Where did Jesus teach his Disciples one day? (Matthew 24:3)

Mt. Gilead
Mt. Seir
Mt. Sinai
Mt. Sinai
Mt. Hor
Mt. Ebal
Mt. Tabor
Mt. Gilboa
Mt. Carmel
Mt. of Olives

YELLOWSTONE NATIONAL PARK

Yellowstone National Park is famous for its two hundred active geysers and thousands of hot springs. Its scenic wonders include cascading waterfalls, steep canyons, verdant meadows and sparkling lakes. Most of Yellowstone's landscape was created by volcanic eruptions. Old Faithful is the best-known geyser in the park. It erupts about every sixty-five minutes, sending a stream of water over one hundred feet into the air. Buffalo, elk, grizzly bears, black bears, cougars, moose, mule deer, bald eagles, and trumpeter swans find refuge in this beautiful park.

MAKE A SAND PICTURE

On a piece of construction paper draw an outline of an animal that lives in Yellowstone Park. Glue brown string to the outline. Color sand with food coloring and allow to dry. Place glue all over the animal and sprinkle it with the colored sand. Allow it to dry for a few minutes, then shake off the excess sand. Use small pieces of felt for the eyes and other features.

OLYMPIC NATIONAL PARK

Throughout Olympic National Park jagged peaks of the Olympic Range reach heavenward. Rain forests of Douglas fir, Sitka spruce, western red cedar and hemlock cover the landscape. Good soil and heavy rainfall make lush undergrowth possible. It is a wonderland of alpine meadows and turbulent streams. Picturesque mosses drape branches and tree trunks. About one thousand varieties of flowers dot the valleys and mountain slopes.

MINIATURE PARK

To capture some of this beauty, have each child make a miniature park in a dish. Select a large enough container to allow for variety. Place small pebbles in the bottom of each dish. Fill each dish with soil, mounding it up on one end to form a mountain. Place small plants and plastic flowers in the little park. Use twigs for trees. Make a road by using pebbles. A mirror will make a good lake. Arrange the items so they are pleasing to the eye.

Shining Star Publications, Copyright © 1987, A division of Good Apple, Inc.   SS843

VOLCANIC WONDERS
CRATER LAKE

Crater Lake is the deepest lake in the United States, some parts being 1,932 feet deep. The lake was formed when Mount Mazama collapsed in a volcanic eruption, leaving a huge bowl which filled with water. There are no known outlets and no streams flowing into the lake. This scenic wonder was made a national park in 1902.

MAKE A VOLCANO

Make a cone from lightweight cardboard. Cover the cardboard with plaster of paris, leaving an opening in the top large enough to hold a half-cup measuring cup. Fill the cup with vinegar and enough baking soda to make the liquid foam and run over the sides.

CRATERS OF THE MOON NATIONAL MONUMENT

Hundreds of years ago lava spewed from the depths of the earth to form the most fantastic landscape one could imagine. When the hot lava cooled, the area resembled the surface of the moon. The landscape is covered with countless caves, huge cracks, and natural bridges. Many of the lava formations resemble birds or other animals. One can detect shapes that look like twisted rope. Many colors are seen throughout the crater. Located in the state of Idaho, it is truly a volcanic wonder. It was established as a national monument in 1924.

THE MIGHTY RIVERS

Flowing 2,348 miles from its source in northern Minnesota to its mouth in the Gulf of Mexico, the Mississippi is the longest river in the United States. The river has been important in the history of our country. It provided transportation for the early trappers and traders. Today, it transports about forty percent of the freight handled by the inland waterways. Its banks are lined with hardwood trees. The river supports many freshwater fish. Mississippi means "Big River." In a famous song it is called "Old Man River." Mark Twain used the Mississippi River as the setting for many of his stories.

Down the river I'll choose to float
In a raft, an inner tube, or a little boat,
Dreaming of a long, long ago day
When trappers and traders passed this way.

WRITE RIVER POETRY

Write four-line verses about the rivers in your area. Illustrate the poems.

THE COLUMBIA RIVER

The Columbia River is one of the important rivers of the western United States. It is 1,214 miles long. The Columbia River provides water for irrigating western farmlands. It also provides hydroelectric power.

Many recreational uses are made of the Columbia River. Make a river mosaic. Have each child draw a river scene with a boat. Cut one-half inch squares of construction paper for the children to use as tiles to fill in the pictures. To distinguish the water from the sky, make sure two shades of blue are available.

MAMMOTH CAVE

Mammoth Cave, the largest single cave in the world, is located in Kentucky. The cave is often called one of the wonders of the Western World because of its huge size and remarkable formations. Some rocks within the cave resemble flowers, trees, and other natural objects.

CHRISTIANS WORSHIPPED IN CAVES

Because early Christians suffered persecution, they often held their services in caves in order to be hidden from the soldiers who were trying to find them. Christians followed paths of drawings of fish to find their way to other believers. Often Christian artists would draw pictures in the caves to show scenes from the life of Christ. Have the children pretend they are early Christians. Draw a scene from the life of Christ that they would not want future generations to forget.

CAVE WRITINGS

Spelunkers often find picture writing within caves that tells about long-ago civilizations. Have the children develop some symbols. Then select a Scripture and write it in picture language. Exchange messages to see if they can be decoded.

- heaven
- cloud
- light
- child
- mountain
- earth
- hear
- see
- sing
- home
- sea
- tree

LONG AGO

Words by Helen Kitchell Evans
Music by Frances Mann Benson

Long be-fore the peo-ple Could stand and view Beau-ty was there, The paint-ed des-ert, Grand Can-yon, too. Great lakes and riv-ers Like the Mis-sis-sip-pi. God placed them there when the earth was new. Oh, God cre-a-ted beau-ty for us to see. Let us give God praise; God is ver-y good to you and me.

32

Shining Star Publications, Copyright © 1987, A division of Good Apple, Inc.

SS843

America! America! God Shed His Grace on Thee

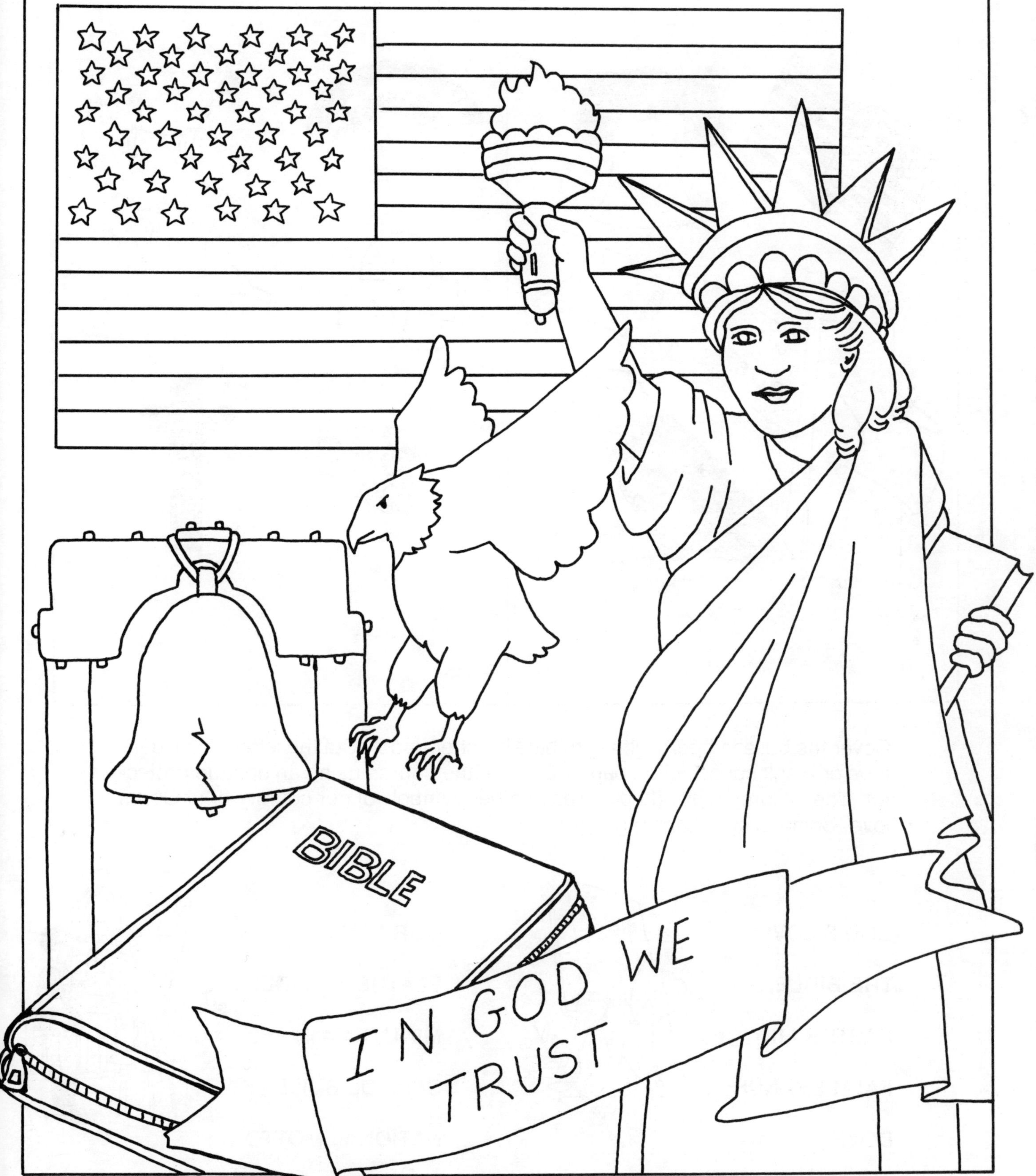

Bulletin Board Idea

SYMBOLS OF OUR LAND

SYMBOLS OF GOD'S LOVE

Cover the bulletin board with light blue butcher paper. Cut the letters from dark blue or black construction paper. Enlarge the figures using an opaque projector. The children may add pictures of other symbols of our country or of God's love. Some suggestions include

GOD'S LOVE

THE BIBLE

EASTER LILY

PALM BRANCH

DOVE

OUR LAND

STATUE OF LIBERTY

MINUTEMAN

CAPITOL BUILDING

NATIONAL MOTTO

RALLY AROUND THE FLAG
PROUDLY IT WAVES

Patriotism is built around our country's flag. The colors of the flag were chosen with care: the white represents freedom, the red stands for courage and the blue is for loyalty. Each star represents one state, while the stripes represent the thirteen colonies.

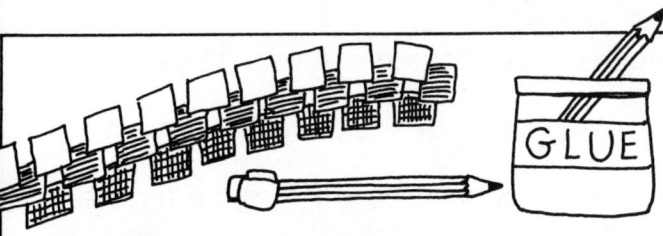

MAKE A CREPE-PAPER FLAG

Provide a large paper outline of the American flag. Cut red, white and blue crepe paper into one-inch square pieces. Have the children wrap the pieces around the eraser end of a pencil. Dip each piece of crepe paper in glue and place it on the flag. Follow this procedure until the entire flag is covered.

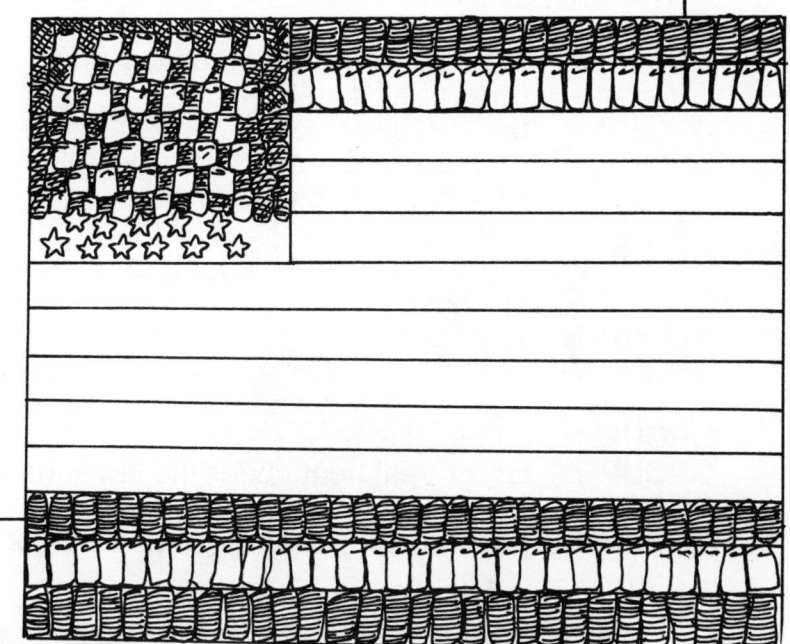

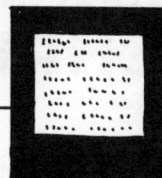

RESPECT THE FLAG

Our flag is a symbol of our country. It represents our ideas of democracy and freedom for all people. The flag by itself is only a piece of cloth, but the makers designed this symbol to have special meaning for all American citizens. Because of the significance the flag holds for the people, it must be treated with respect and care. To learn about the proper use of the American flag, obtain free copies of **How to Display and Respect the American Flag of the United States**, a publication available from any naval recruiting office. To make a learning center from these pamphlets, cut the pictures out and mount them on red construction paper. The information that describes each picture should also be cut separately and mounted on red construction paper. Place all of the pictures on the learning center board. Children should be able to match the word descriptions to the various pictures.

A CHORAL READING FOR THE PLEDGE OF ALLEGIANCE

GROUP 1:   I pledge allegiance
GROUP 2:   I make a promise.
GROUP 1:   to the flag
GROUP 2:   The symbol that represents the democracy we all enjoy.
GROUP 1:   of the United States of America
GROUP 2:   The country that was founded by brave men who wanted everyone to be free.
GROUP 1:   and to the Republic for which it stands,
GROUP 2:   The nation that was established for the people and by the people.
GROUP 1:   one Nation
GROUP 2:   Fifty individual states united under one national government working for the good of all its citizens.
GROUP 1:   under God,
GROUP 2:   As our Creator and Father we give allegiance to the one God who has made freedom possible.
GROUP 1:   indivisible,
GROUP 2:   Our country has pledged to work together to solve differences which would divide us.
GROUP 1:   with liberty
GROUP 2:   Freedom to worship, freedom to speak, freedom to write, freedom to assemble with any group and freedom to choose any vocation.
GROUP 1:   and justice
GROUP 2:   Equal treatment under the law—the right to be judged fairly.
GROUP 1:   for all.
GROUP 2:   Each person, regardless of his background, education, religion or wealth.

A CHORAL READING FOR THE PLEDGE TO THE CHRISTIAN FLAG

GROUP 1:   I pledge allegiance
GROUP 2:   I promise to be faithful
GROUP 1:   to the Christian flag
GROUP 2:   The symbol which represents the people who obey the commandments of Christ.
GROUP 1:   and to the Savior
GROUP 2:   Jesus who died to pay the penalty for our sins.
GROUP 1:   for whose Kingdom it stands,
GROUP 2:   All people on earth who are in harmony with God.
GROUP 1:   one brotherhood
GROUP 2:   All nations and races are combined to form one family in God.
GROUP 1:   uniting all mankind
GROUP 2:   Racial differences are dissolved when the love of God shines through.
GROUP 1:   in service
GROUP 2:   Each one working to help a brother or sister along the way.
GROUP 1:   and love.
GROUP 2:   God is love. He commands us to love one another even as He loves us.

THE NATIONAL ANTHEM

Songs can be used to strengthen the ties of friendship and the bonds of love each citizen has for America. "The Star-Spangled Banner" was written by a young lawyer in 1814. Frances Scott Key watched from a ship as Fort McHenry was being bombarded by the enemy in a night-long siege. In the dawn, as light brightened the horizon, Francis Scott Key could see that the American flag was still flying. He was so stirred emotionally by the sight of the flag and the brave soldiers who had fought to defend it, that he wrote the poem which provides the words for our national anthem. The music was added later. Although the song was very popular, it was not declared the official anthem until March 3, 1931.

Learn all of the verses of "The Star-Spangled Banner." This song is easier for young children to role-play than to sing. As the words are read by the teacher, the children may act out the words.

THE CHRISTIAN ANTHEM

The Christian faith does not have one song that unites it. There are many songs that individuals consider special. Have a contest to find one song that the children and their parents would like to have as the Christian anthem.

FIRST PATRIOTIC SONG

Early American soldiers were an odd-looking assortment. They had no uniforms. Some wore coonskin caps and moccasins. Others had floppy coats and deerskin leggings. The British, who had splendid uniforms, often made fun of the American soldiers. They called them "Yankee Doodles." Yankee meant that they were Americans. Doodle was a British word that meant "ridiculous" or "do-nothing." The British made up the song "Yankee Doodle." However, the American soldiers liked the catchy tune so well that they began singing it. Over the years many verses have been added to the song. Have the children make up some of their own, selecting events in recent history as the basis for the new words.

GOD IS HONORED IN AMERICA'S GREAT SEAL

People see the Great Seal of the United States almost every day, but no one gives it much thought. It appears on the back side of dollar bills.

A committee began working on the seal July 4, 1776. Thomas Jefferson, Benjamin Franklin, and John Adams were some of the men who served on the committee to design it. In 1789 the present seal was adopted by Congress.

FRONT SIDE OF THE SEAL

Every part of the Great Seal is important. At the top of the front side, there is a circular design called the crest. America was seen as a new constellation in the sky, so stars make up this portion. The number of stars represents the thirteen original colonies. The ring of light which breaks through the white cloud symbolizes God's guidance and protection of America. The eagle symbolizes strength. The shield of the United States is shown on the body of the eagle. The words on the banner in the eagle's beak mean "One out of many." This refers to all the states which make up our country. The eagle holds the olive branch to symbolize peace. It also has a bundle of arrows to show that the country will defend its freedom in time of war.

BACK SIDE OF THE SEAL

The back side of the seal features a pyramid, an eye and two mottoes. The pyramid is a symbol of the strength of our government. The pyramid was left unfinished to represent the fact that the country will continue to grow in many ways. The eye represents God's watchful care of the nation. The light around the eye reminds us of the glory of God. The words over the eye mean "God has favored this undertaking." The motto under the pyramid means "A new order of the ages."

GOD'S EYE

One of the symbols of God is an eye placed in a triangle. It is called the All-Seeing Eye. It is shown on the back of American dollar bills, as explained on the previous page. Churches in England put the symbol on the wall behind the pulpit. In times past a minister would sometimes misuse the symbol by telling the congregation that God was searching for their sins so He could punish them. Other people view this eye as a symbol of the loving Father, who is always guarding His precious creation. When it is viewed in this manner, it is a symbol of joy and comfort.

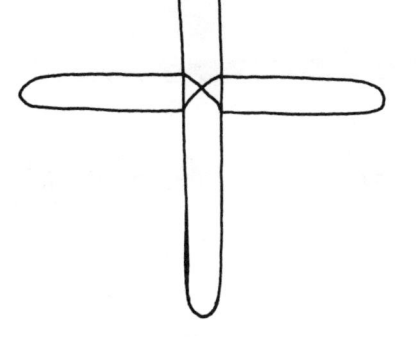

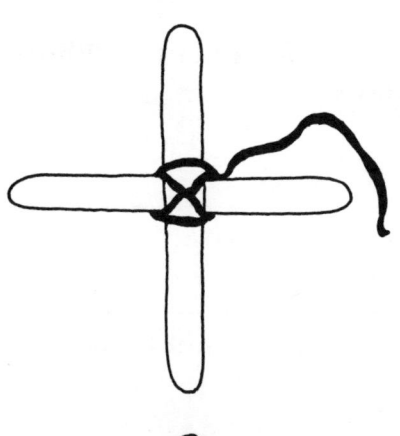

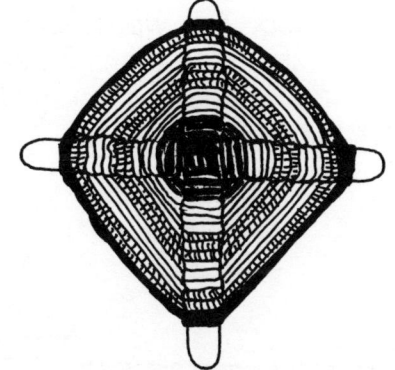

MAKE A GOD'S EYE

1. Tie two sticks together to form a cross.
2. Starting at the center, weave yarn over and under the sticks until the yarn is at the outside edges of the sticks.
3. Cut the yarn and glue the end in place.
4. Make a loop at the top so it can be hung on the wall.

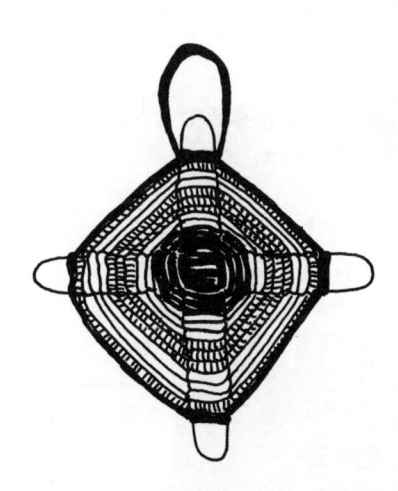

Shining Star Publications, Copyright © 1987, A division of Good Apple, Inc.

SS843

THE STATUE OF LIBERTY
SYMBOL OF FRIENDSHIP

The Statue of Liberty was a gift from the people of France. It was designed as a symbol of the friendship established when France helped America during the Revolutionary War. The French people agreed to cover the cost of making the statue. The American people raised money to pay for the pedestal. From the base of the pedestal the statue towers over three hundred feet in the air. No wonder it took Auguste Bartholdi ten years to build it. He called the statue "Liberty Enlightening the World." Many songs and poems have been written about it. One poem written by Emma Lazarus in 1883 ends with these famous lines:

Give me your tired, your poor,
Your huddled masses yearning to breathe free,
The wretched refuse of your teeming shore.
Send these, the homeless, tempest-tost to me,
I lift my lamp beside the golden door!

Learn this portion of the poem. Also learn about true liberty from II Corinthians 3:17 ". . . where the Spirit of the Lord is, there is Liberty."

DESIGN A NEW STATUE

Mr. Bartholdi had to think a long time about how he would design his statue to represent liberty. Think of another virtue like kindness, friendliness, love, compassion or devotion to God and your country. Design a statue that would symbolize these ideals. Draw it for others to see. Or it could be made from clay.

LIBERTY AWARD

_____

has learned the poem of liberty and I Corinthians 3:17.

on _____

_____
Teacher

THE NATIONAL BIRD
THE BALD EAGLE

The bald eagle is our national bird. However, not everyone was pleased with this choice. Benjamin Franklin wanted the wild turkey to be our national bird. He thought the eagle had been the symbol used by too many other countries.

THE MAJESTIC BIRD

The eagle is a majestic bird, measuring about forty inches in length. The wingspread can be eight feet. It weighs between eight and twelve pounds. The eagle eats small animals, fish, snakes and other birds. It makes its huge nest in high trees or on cliffs. The nest is sometimes eight feet wide and eight feet deep. The eagle is not really bald, but it appears that way because it has a white head.

"But they that wait upon the Lord shall renew their strength; they shall mount up with wings as eagles; they shall run, and not be weary; and they shall walk, and not faint."
Isaiah 40:31

MAKE A STENCIL PRINT

1. Make a copy of the eagle. (see page 42)
2. Cut out the dark portions.
3. Lay the stencil on art paper. Tape it in place.
4. Use thick paints or crayons to color the cutout sections. When using paint be careful not to get the brush too wet, or the paint will seep into the wrong sections of the drawing.
5. Allow the paint to dry.
6. Carefully remove the top pattern.

EAGLE STENCIL

UNCLE SAM

Many stories have been circulated about the origin of Uncle Sam. Many people believe that the original Uncle Sam was Sam Wilson, who was a government inspector during the War of 1812. After approving the military supplies, he would stamp U.S. on them. The initials stood for United States, but many people began to joke that they stood for Uncle Sam. Soon cartoonists began drawing pictures of Uncle Sam. It was not long before Uncle Sam became a national symbol.

MAKE A HAT FOR UNCLE SAM

The hat can be made from an oatmeal box. Cover the empty box with white construction paper. Cut a circle of white construction paper for the top. Glue it onto the box. Cut narrow strips of red construction paper to form the stripes and glue them on the hat from top to bottom. Make a hat brim from a circle of lightweight cardboard. From the center, cut slits to form an opening for the head. Fold the slits and glue into the inside of the oatmeal box to hold the rim in place. Make a blue band with white stars. Glue this to the base of the hat just above the rim.

IN GOD WE TRUST

The motto of our country is inscribed on our coins and documents to remind us that our country was established by people who believed in God. Have the children make a shield showing how they trust in God.

BE PATRIOTIC

Make three-foot-high letters spelling **AMERICA**. Have the children draw brightly colored scenes of events or places in America on 8" x 11" paper. Glue these scenes onto the large letters. Cut around the edges from the back side so that the scenes fit the letters. Display on a large wall in the hall or as a backdrop for a patriotic program. (See page 143 for the play **Celebrate America**.)

Shining Star Publications, Copyright © 1987, A division of Good Apple, Inc.   SS843

SYMBOLS OF THE CHURCH

As our country has symbols which characterize the nation, so the church has emblems which depict it. The fish represented a Christian in the early days. Christians were not permitted to meet publicly, because their religion was not approved by the emperor. They had to meet secretly. They used the fish symbol to let other people know they were Christians; or they drew the fish symbol on the ground to find out if an individual was a Christian. This symbol was used because the Greek letters which spell fish are the first letters in the Greek language for words which mean Jesus Christ, Son of God, Savior.

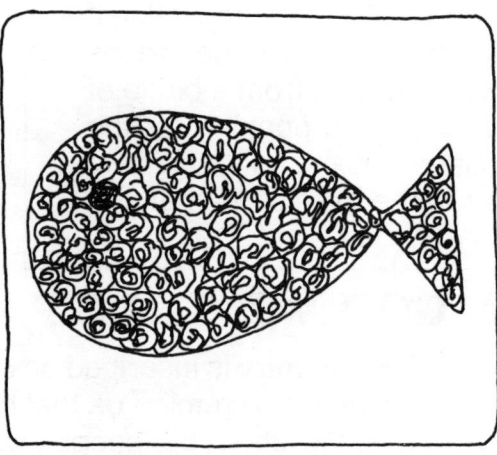

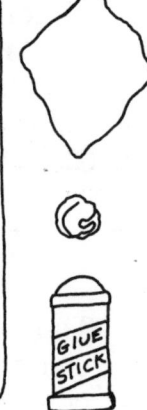

MAKE FISH SYMBOLS

Draw an outline of a fish on the inside of a grocer's meat tray. Cut small pieces of tissue paper and roll into small balls. Glue the balls onto the fish shape, covering it completely. Use black tissue paper for the eye. The meat tray will form the frame for the picture.

THE RAINBOW IS A SYMBOL OF PROMISE

The story of this symbol is found in Genesis, chapters 6-9. There are other symbols in this story which we still use today. The dove with the olive branch in its mouth is a symbol of peace. The ark is a symbol of safety. The rainbow symbolizes God's promise that He would never again destroy the earth with water. It is also a symbol of God's love and protection. Find other symbols of our religious beliefs.

And Crown Thy Good with Brotherhood From Sea to Shining Sea

Bulletin Board Idea

ONE NATION UNDER GOD

Cover the board with white butcher paper. Make the letters dark blue. Enlarge the figures and place them around the Bible and the map of the United States. The children may add items to the board which show what our country obtained from each of the different cultures.

AMERICAN INDIANS
THE FIRST AMERICANS

The first Americans were the Indians. By the time America was being settled by the Europeans, there were approximately one million Indians in the country. The Indians divided themselves into tribes. Each tribe had its own language and way of life. Some Indians lived in permanent villages, raising their own food in gardens. Other tribes wandered from place to place in search of food. Homes and clothing also differed among tribes.

The Pueblo Indians lived in adobe houses.

MAKE A PUEBLO HOUSE

Obtain small boxes of various sizes. Cut holes for the windows and doors. Flatten clay to about ¼" thickness. Cover the boxes with the clay, pinching the corners together. Stack the boxes to make three or four levels, with the smaller boxes on top. Make ladders to get from one level to another from twigs or Popsicle sticks.

INDIANS LIKED TO PLAY

Indians of different tribes played a variety of games. They loved to dance and sing. Indians danced for special ceremonies, to celebrate victories, or just for fun. Some tribes played a game similar to soccer. An animal skin was stuffed and sewn together. The players then kicked the ball back and forth across the ground.

A favorite toy of several tribes was a "hummer."

MAKE A HUMMER

The Indians carved a piece of wood for their game. You can use a large button. Decorate the button with painted geometric shapes. Cut two triangles from cardboard. Glue them opposite one another on the button. Cut a heavy string about thirty-six inches long, thread it through the buttonholes, and tie a knot in it. Twirl the string until it is tight. Then pull the string out as far as it will go. Relax the string. Continue doing this. Listen for the humming sound.

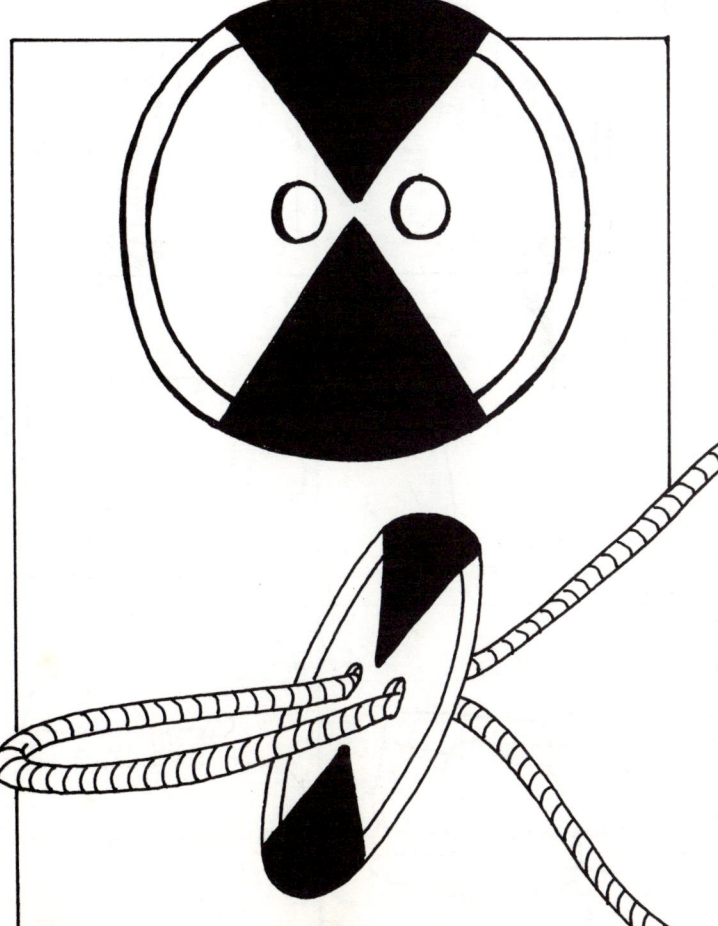

MAKE AN INDIAN SHIRT

1. Have child stand with outstretched arms and measure him from wrist to wrist.
2. Measure the length of the arms.
3. Measure from the shoulder to just below the knee.
4. Using these measurements make a pattern as shown.
5. Cut two pieces of felt, using the pattern as a guide.
6. Cut the front in two from top to bottom.
7. Sew the front and back sections together at the shoulder and underarm seams.
8. Cut a 2" fringe along the bottom of sleeves and bottom of the shirt.
9. Cut a 3" strip of felt to go around the shoulders. Fringe this and glue it to the shirt.

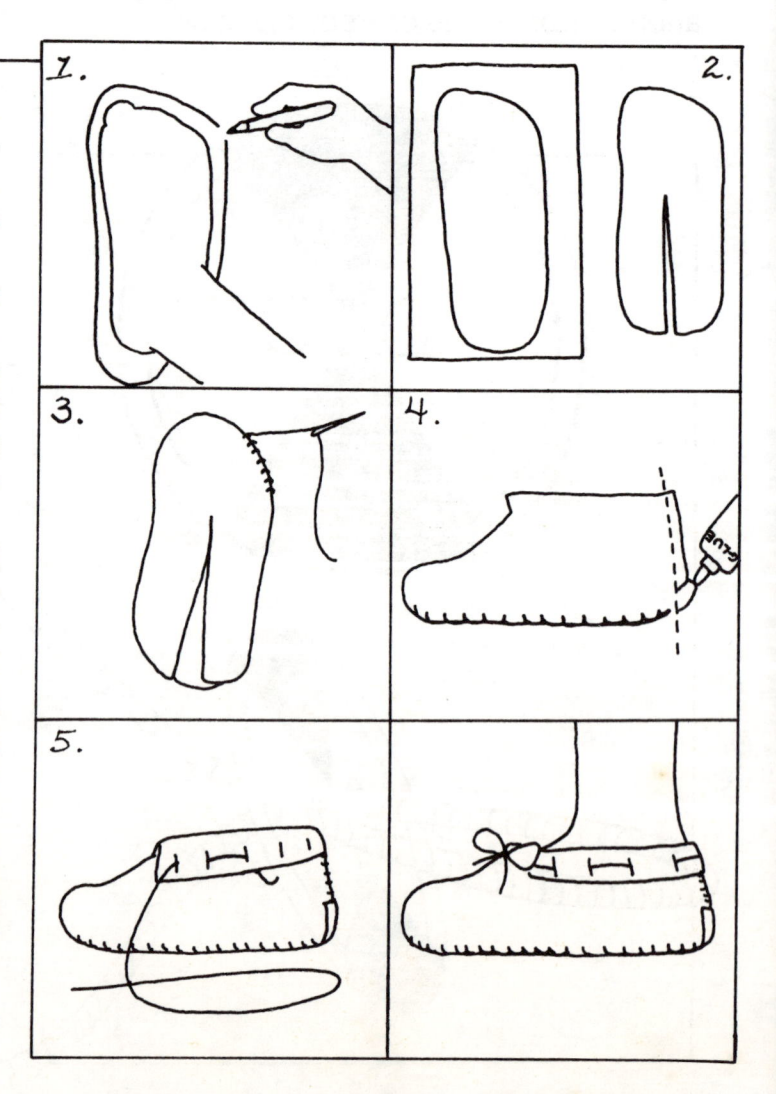

MAKE SOME MOCCASINS

1. Place the foot on a piece of newsprint. Trace around it, leaving at least one extra inch around the sides and front. Leave about two inches in the back. Use this for a pattern.
2. Lay the pattern on felt material. Cut around it. Make four pieces this size. The two pieces that will form the tops should be cut two-thirds of the way down the center from the back side. The front third of the moccasin should not be cut.
3. Place a top and bottom together. Sew around the outside edges. Leave the back side free.
4. Slip the foot in to determine the size. Bring the back two edges together. Cut off the excess. Whipstitch or glue this part in place. Bring the bottom section up the back and stitch into place.
5. Turn top edge down to form a cuff. Make vertical slits along this section about 1½" from the top. Thread a cord through these slits to hold the moccasins on the feet.

¿HABLA USTED ESPAÑOL?

One of the largest ethnic groups in the United States is the Hispanics. These people speak the Spanish language. Some of them are from Mexico, Puerto Rico, Cuba and some South American countries.

The people share many traditions even though they come from different countries. Christmas, or **La Navidad**, is one of the happiest holidays. They also celebrate **El Dia de los Reyes**—The Day of the Kings—representing the day the wise men visited Jesus. To celebrate the occasion, the children leave their shoes on the doorstep on the night of January 5th. The next morning they find presents by the shoes.

LAS POSADAS

Las Posadas is a little play in which the people travel from house to house. It is a tradition of the Hispanic people. Posada means shelter. In this play the actors are pretending to be Mary and Joseph, as they search for a place to stay in Bethlehem. At the first house they are turned away, but the people join them and go on to other houses. At the last house they are invited to enter, and the group has a party. Often a pinata is a part of the festivities.

Role-play this traditional event with the children.

THE PINATA IS A TRADITION

Another Hispanic tradition is the making of a pinata. A pinata is a clay pot or paper container decorated to look like an animal or other object. The pinata is filled with candy, gum and small trinkets or toys. A child is blindfolded and tries to hit the pinata with a stick. When the pinata is broken, all of the goodies scatter to the floor. The children scramble and gather them.

MAKE A PINATA

YOU WILL NEED
1 large balloon
Red and yellow butcher paper
Laundry starch
Old newspapers
Light rope or heavy cord
Gummed stars
Scissors

Inflate the balloon to about 12" in diameter. Tie it shut.

Tear the newspapers into 2" strips. (Tearing rather than cutting will make a stronger pinata.)

Dip the newspapers into the laundry starch. Cover the balloon from top to bottom with overlapping strips, leaving an opening at the top. Cover the balloon again, going around it this time. Finish by placing two more layers from top to bottom. Allow this to dry, then pop the balloon.

Glue the rope to the pinata.

Cut the butcher paper into 3" strips. Fold the strips lengthwise. Make 1" slits along the folded edge.

Pull each of these sections over the scissors blade to curl them.

Glue these sections to the pinata, placing the ruffles close together. Alternate two rows of red and two rows of yellow. It would be simpler to make the pinata all one color if the children are doing this part by themselves.

Decorate the pinata with the stars.

Fill the finished pinata by placing goodies into the top hole. Have a pinata party!

FRANCE HELPS AMERICA WIN ITS FREEDOM

In 1777 the French, who had a strong navy, decided to help the struggling little country of America in the war against the British. The French Navy was able to cut off the British ships so fresh supplies could not be brought to the soldiers. In the summer of 1781, General Cornwallis moved his army to Yorktown, Virginia, a town which was surrounded on three sides by water. The French Navy was able to defeat the British. Cornwallis surrendered to George Washington. A peace treaty was signed in Paris, France, which gave the American colonies their independence from Great Britian.

Have the children write a thank-you note to the country of France for helping us to attain our freedom.

SOME FRENCHMEN SEEK RELIGIOUS FREEDOM

The French Huguenots were being persecuted in their own country because they did not follow the religious beliefs of the rulers. They came to America to find religious freedom.

Some famous French Hugenots were Paul Revere, Priscilla Mullins and Henry Wadsworth Longfellow. Read one of Longfellow's famous writings, ''The Courtship of Miles Standish.''

FRENCH ART FORM

Pointillism is a French art form. It is a technique whereby many little dots of color are placed close together. The eye of the viewer then can visually put the dots together to form the intended shape. This can be done by using the point of a crayon. Provide each child with a paper containing the outline of an animal. Using only the point of the crayon, make small dots until the picture is colored. The dots should blend together when one looks at the picture from a short distance.

THE FRENCH GAVE US APRIL FOOLS' DAY

The holiday we call April Fools' Day was started long ago. It is believed to have originated in France in 1564 when a new calendar was adopted. Up to this time New Year's Day was celebrated by giving gifts to family and friends on April 1. When the calendar changed, some people did not accept the idea. Others simply forgot the change and continued with their former practices. Their friends made fun of them by sending silly presents on April 1. England and America accepted the new calendar in 1754. The practice of catching April Fools continued in America because everyone liked the day for the fun it produced.

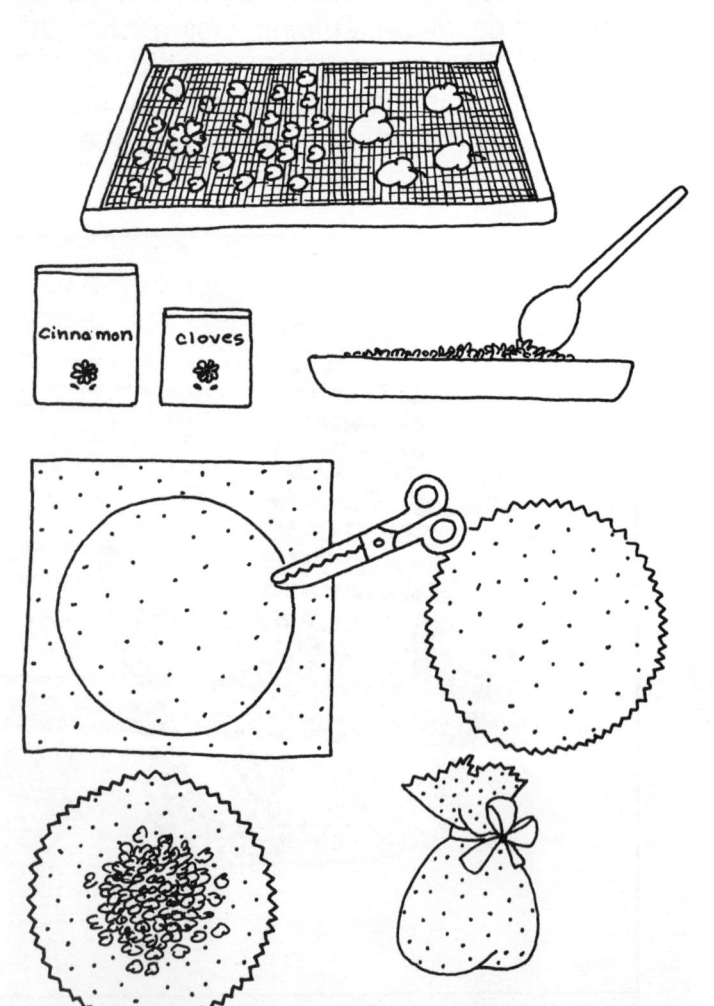

AHHHH-FRAGRANT PERFUMES

The French are known for their fragrant perfumes. Ladies have always loved sweet fragrances. Even in Bible times sweet-smelling ointments were used. Before Esther was presented to King Ahasuerus, she used oil of myrrh for six months; and then she used other fragrant ointments for another six months. Read about this story in Esther 2. The French brought some of their perfume-making skill to America. Try making a simple sachet.

ROSE SACHET

1. Pick some rose petals in the morning.
2. Snip some leaves from a geranium plant.
3. Dry the leaves and petals on a wire rack until they are easily crumbled.
4. Add some cinnamon and cloves to the petals and leaves. Mix this combination thoroughly.
5. Using pinking shears, cut a circle of soft fabric about 5 inches in diameter.
6. Place the crumbled leaves and petals in the center of the fabric.
7. Tie the sachet with a narrow ribbon.

JEWS IN AMERICA— GOD'S CHOSEN PEOPLE

". . . I will make of thee a great nation, and I will bless thee, and make thy name great; and thou shalt be a blessing . . . and in thee shall all families of the earth be blessed." Genesis 12:2,3

Jews have lived in almost every land on the earth. The first Jews came to America from Spain, seeking religious freedom. The Jewish people observe their traditions wherever they go.

BAR MITZVAH BAT MITZVAH

From birth the Jewish child is taught the traditions of his religious faith. The child also memorizes passages from the Bible. On the child's thirteenth birthday a change takes place, representing his or her passage into adulthood and the assumption of accompanying religious responsibilities. The ritual for a boy is called the **bar mitzvah** and for a girl, the **bat mitzvah**. During the ceremony the birthday child has the opportunity to explain some portion of the Torah or a facet of Jewish life. Afterwards a festive birthday party is given.

THE JEWS HAVE A SPECIAL CALENDAR

If you look on a Jewish calendar, you might become very confused. It is quite different from the one to which we are accustomed. The world calendar is based on the earth's movement around the sun. The Jewish calendar is based on the movements of the moon. It is called a lunar calendar. The new month begins with the new moon, and the year is only 354 days long. To make up the difference, an extra month is added every few years. Find out when the next Jewish month will begin. Check for the new moon.

LOOK AT THE JEWISH YEARS

The year on our calendar will be different from the one on the Jewish calendar. Christians count the years from the birth of Christ; Jews count the years from the time of creation. Their year is 3760 higher in number than ours. Calculate the present Jewish year. 1987 + 3760 =

Calculate the year of your birth, using the Jewish calendar.

JEWS CELEBRATE THE SABBATH

"And God blessed the seventh day, and sanctified it: because that in it he had rested from all his work which God created and made." Genesis 2:3

The Jews still observe the seventh day as the day of rest. Their Sabbath begins on Friday evening at sundown and it lasts until sundown on Saturday. On Friday evening the Sabbath candles are lit, and Jewish families prepare for a day of rest. They want to follow this commandment:

"Remember the sabbath day, to keep it holy." Exodus 20:8

On the Sabbath, families go to the synagogue to worship.

JEWS CELEBRATE PURIM

When the holiday of Purim is celebrated, Jews take noisemakers to the synagogue. On this occasion the book of Esther is read. Every time the name of Haman is mentioned, the children sound their noisemakers and stamp their feet. Haman was a man who tried to kill all the Jews, but Esther helped to prevent him from doing this terrible deed. After the book of Esther is read, Jewish people enjoy treats called hamantaschen. They are fruit-filled pastries which are folded to look like Haman's hat.

To get a feeling for this Jewish holiday, read the book of Esther and allow the children to react noisily when Haman's name is read. Then make hamentaschen.

HAMANTASCHEN

DOUGH
¾ cup sugar
2 cups flour
2 tsp. baking powder
¼ tsp. salt
⅓ cup butter
1 egg
2 T. water

Mix the first 4 ingredients. Cut in the butter with a pastry blender. Mix until crumbly. Add egg and water to form a ball. Roll the dough out on a floured surface to about 1/8" thickness. Using a glass, cut circles from the dough. Place a tablespoon of filling in the center of each circle. Fold the edges of the circle to the middle, forming a triangle. Place the triangles on a greased cookie sheet. Bake at 350° for 20 minutes. Makes about 2 dozen.

FILLING
1 apple
1 pound cooked pitted prunes
2 tsp. honey

Chop the prunes finely. Grate the apple. Mix the fruits with the honey.

Other fruits or fruit pie filling may be used. Nuts could also be added.

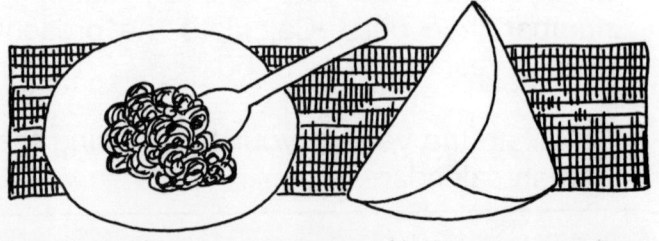

ITALIANS IN AMERICA

Italians did not begin coming to America in large numbers until after 1880. However, Italians were very important in our early history. It was an Italian named Christopher Columbus who discovered the New World. Our continent's name comes from Amerigo Vespucci, an Italian who sailed for the country of Spain in 1499. He was the first to realize that Columbus had not found a new route to the Far East, but had discovered a new continent.

AMERICA NEEDS WORKERS

In the late 1800's, Italy had become heavily populated, and the southern farmland was being depleted. Meanwhile in America, great industrial advances had been made. Workers were needed. Many Italians were brought to America by labor contractors. Life was hard for the Italian immigrants, but they worked hard to become good citizens. They brought many foods with them that Americans did not have. They introduced broccoli, zucchini squash, endive and Italian grapes to our diet. Probably the most popular Italian food, however, is the pizza pie. Here is a simple pizza recipe.

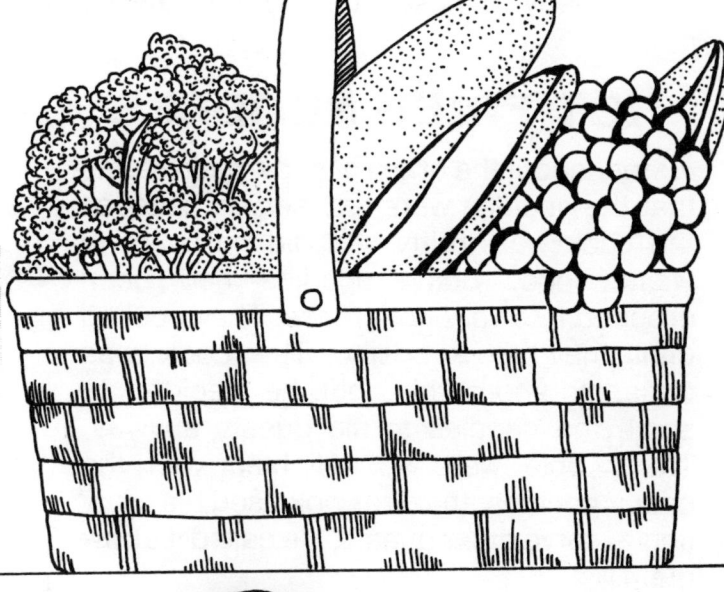

PIZZA FOR ONE CHILD
1 slice bread, English muffin, or slice of French bread
Tomato sauce or pizza sauce
Oregano
White cheese
Garlic powder

Toast one side of the bread in a toaster oven. Place thinly sliced white cheese on the toasted side of the bread. Make sure it comes out to the edges. Spread about a tablespoon of tomato sauce over the cheese. Sprinkle lightly with oregano and garlic powder. Place this in the toaster oven and cook until the cheese melts.

ITALIANS LOVE MUSIC

Italians brought their love of music with them to the new world. Many of the musical terms we use are from the Italian language. **Solo** means alone. **Presto** means quickly. **Forte** and **fortissimo** are Italian words which mean loud and very loud. The names for some of our instruments are Italian: **violin**, **cello**, and **piano**. The word **opera** is also Italian. Opera is singing drama, first composed by the Italians. Have the children go through music books and list as many Italian musical terms as they can.

CHINESE INGENUITY

Many Chinese people came to America to seek work. They planned to work hard and save enough money to go home and buy some land for their families. Because they intended to stay for only a short time, they did not bring their families. Finding work was hard. Many worked on the western section of the Central Pacific Railroad (which met with the eastern section at Promontory Point in Utah). They worked hard and many lost their lives because the jobs were hazardous. Even though their wages were poor, many Chinese wished to own their own businesses. Because it took little money to open a laundry, many Chinese laundries appeared across the country.

HOT FRIED NOODLES

A story about the origin of chow mein states that the noodles were first served because the cook was thrifty and did not want to waste food. Some noodles had been dropped into very hot grease. They cooked until they were crispy. The cook was unhappy about this, but he decided to serve the noodles to his guests anyway. The people were so delighted with the crispy noodles, that the cook used his creation to serve other guests. He called it **chow mein**.

CHINESE LOVE DELICATE ARTWORK

Beautiful scenes with soft colors are evident in Chinese artwork. The Chinese decorate simply, but beautifully. They love fans. Make a fan by drawing a scene on a piece of construction paper. Fold the paper into accordion-style pleats. Tape the bottom of the fan to hold the pleats in place.

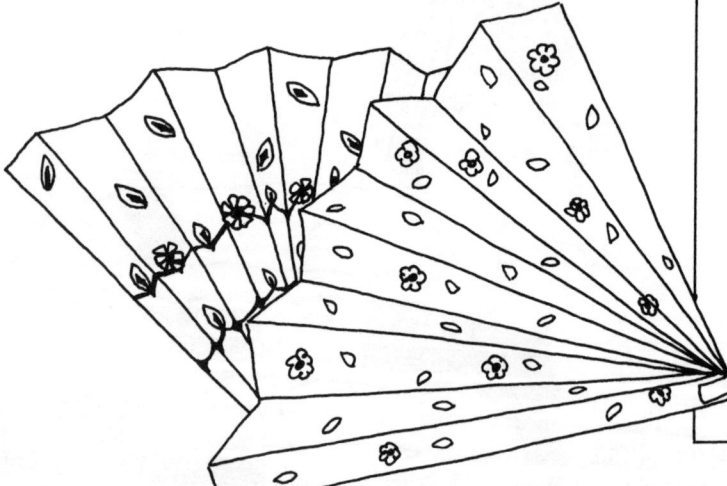

CHOP SUEY AND CHOW MEIN ARE NOT REALLY CHINESE DISHES

These main dishes were unknown in China, and there are many stories about the origin of these foods. One story states that chop suey was first prepared by Chinese cooks in California. Some rough gold miners had come into a restaurant late at night. The cooks had to prepare them something to keep them calm. They tossed together the items they had on hand in the kitchen. The miners liked the concoction, which the Chinese labeled **chop suey**.

CHINESE TANGRAM

The Chinese have given us mathematical puzzles called **tangrams**. The tangram is made of seven geometric shapes: a rhomboid, a square and five triangles. These shapes can be arranged in dozens of ways to form many objects. People all around the world have been fascinated with the challenge of solving tangram puzzles. Try your skill with this tangram:

THE JAPANESE BRING THEIR SKILLS TO AMERICA

Japanese people did not come to America until about 1890. For many years their country's government forbade emigration. However, Commodore Perry's visit to Japan helped bring about a gradual relaxation of its regulations about foreign travel. Many Japanese came to America because they heard stories of the great wealth of Americans. When they arrived, however, they found only low-paying jobs. Many of them worked in the fruit and vegetable farms in California. In spite of this beginning, the Japanese people have worked hard to find their rightful place in American society. They brought many beautiful customs with them from their country to enrich our country.

JAPANESE POETRY

Haiku is a form of Japanese poetry. A Haiku poem has three lines, with five syllables in the first, seven syllables in the second and five syllables in the third. The subject is usually nature. Try writing Haiku.

PLAY A JAPANESE GAME

JAN KEN PON

Two people play this game using their hands. The players shake their fists up and down three times, saying "**Jan Ken Pon**." Then they stretch out their hands to show stone, paper or scissors. A fist is a stone. A hand with all five fingers out flat is paper. Two fingers out represents scissors.

Scissors win over paper because scissors can cut paper. Stone wins over scissors because a stone can break scissors. Paper wins over stone because it can wrap around a stone.

If both players place their hands in the same position, they repeat the game. This game can be used to determine who goes first in another game or who is "it" in a game.

IN SEARCH OF RELIGIOUS FREEDOM

Many religious groups came to America so that they could worship God in their own way. Most of these groups have changed drastically since their arrival. The Amish, however, have maintained their value system and traditions throughout the years, keeping their lives simple and nearly self-sufficient. The people waste very little. They help one another. They teach their children to love God. They also teach them to respect the land which God has given them.

II Corinthians 6:17 forms a basis for the Amish way of life. "Wherefore come out from among them, and be ye separate . . . ."

Viewing their culture, with few modern conveniences, plain clothing and an emphasis on the value of work, is like traveling back in time. In many ways the Amish way of life may prove to be better than our modern ways. Family ties are very strong; and the Amish cooperate with one another in big and little projects.

A CLASS PROJECT

To show the value of cooperation, have a class quilting project. Ask each child to bring a 6" x 6" square of fabric from home, on which he may sew or draw any design. Each one should sign his name on the piece. When the quilt blocks have been brought to school, arrange them in an artistic pattern and let the children hand sew them together to make a friendship quilt. The finished quilt will make a wonderful gift for principal, school secretary, etc.

HEX SIGNS OF THE AMISH

The Amish who live in Pennsylvania paint **hex signs** on their buildings. Years ago, they believed that the signs brought them good fortune and warded off the evil around them. Today, the signs are used mostly for ornamental purposes. The basis for the hex sign is a star. It may have only four points or as many as thirty-two. Each of the designs has special meaning.

A five-pointed star protects the building from lightning. It also is thought to bring good health to the people.

A six-pointed star represents hope for a good marriage.

A twelve-pointed star is a symbol of wisdom.

MAKE A HEX SIGN

1. Using a compass, draw a double circle.
2. Draw two inner circles.
3. Using a ruler, draw a five-pointed star, as shown.
4. Add other five-pointed stars to the design.
5. Color the sign, using only red, white, yellow and black.

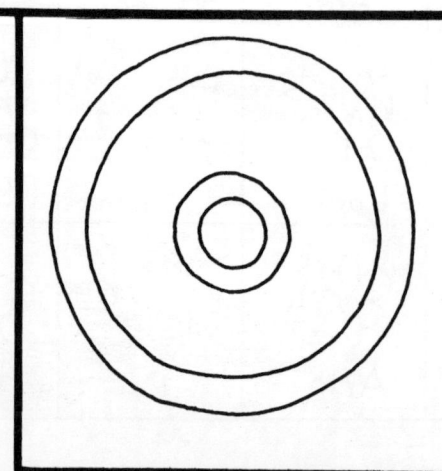

BLACKS IN AMERICA

One group of people did not come to America for freedom. Instead, they arrived in bondage. The first twenty blacks in America were brought by Dutch traders and were sold to the colonists as indentured servants, who were to work for their owners for five to seven years. After this time, they would be free. However, the need for cheap labor grew, and black people were taken forcibly from their homes in Africa and brought to America to be slaves for life. By 1700 there were about 25,000 slaves in the United States. Some had good masters; many had cruel masters. No black man or women had much hope for freedom.

LEARN A NEGRO SPIRITUAL

To bolster their morale during very difficult times, the slaves sang. Theirs were songs that related the plight of the Negro slave to the tribulations of the Israelites under Pharaoh. **Negro spirituals** usually reflected the great faith the black people had in God.

Learn the words to this spiritual, which described the feelings of the black people.

TROUBLE
Trouble, trouble, trouble,
Done had trouble all my days.
Trouble, trouble, trouble,
Done had trouble all my days.
Seems, boys, like dese troubles
Gwine to carry me to my grave.

HARRIET TUBMAN

Harriet Tubman was called the Moses of her people because she led nearly three hundred black people to freedom. Harriet was born into slavery in 1821. She worked as a field hand. She believed it was against God's will to be in bondage. In 1849 Harriet escaped and went to Philadelphia. Friends in the city told her about the **Underground Railroad**, a group of people who hid slaves during their journey to freedom. The individuals who helped the slaves get from one "station" to another were known as "conductors." Harriet served as a conductor, risking her life many times to assist her people.

GOD OF EVERYONE
Words by Helen Kitchell Evans
Music by Frances Mann Benson

1. See our fa-ces and our hands, Our par-ents came from dif-fer-ent lands; God loves all of us we know For our Bi-ble tells us so.
2. You and I look dif-fer-ent, too, Yet we are all the same; God loves ev-ery-one of us, He can call each by his/her name.
3. I am Span-ish, I am French, I am black — Chi-nese; We are ver-y dif-fer-rent, And God loves all of these.
4. We are all A-mer-i-cans, In a coun-try that is grand; Ev-ery race and creed; God bless our na-tive land.

62

Shining Star Publications, Copyright © 1987, A division of Good Apple, Inc.   SS843

*O Beautiful for Pilgrim Feet
Whose Stern Impassion'd Stress*

Bulletin Board Idea

THEY LED THE WAY TO RELIGIOUS FREEDOM

I ENJOY MY RELIGIOUS FREEDOM

Cover the bulletin board with light blue butcher paper. Enlarge the figures and place them on the board. Have the children illustrate ways they use their religious freedom today. Display these pictures on the bottom portion of the bulletin board.

PILGRIM CHILDREN

The Mayflower carried the "Pilgrim Fathers," but it also carried many children. Among the thirty children on board were the Allertons. Bartholomew was 8 years old, Mary was 4, and Remember was 6. Love Brewster was 9, and Wrestling Brewster was 6. The Hopkins children were Constance 14, Giles 12, Damaris 3, and Oceanus, who was born en route. Henry Sampson was 6, and Resolved White was 5. The children shared in the triumphs of the trip as well as in anxious moments.

WRITE A DIARY

Have your students pretend to be Mayflower children and write a diary for the trip. Some items that might be included:
- the emotions felt when leaving Holland,
- the excitement of going out to sea,
- the rocking of the boat during the storm,
- the fears encountered when a beam broke on the ship,
- the day John Howland was rescued after being swept overboard,
- the dreary diet,
- family prayers,
- how they passed the time,
- their feelings when they set foot on the new land.

A BABY IS BORN

Though the ocean trip was very hard for the Pilgrims, some very exciting events occurred. One day a baby was born to the Hopkins family. Many suggestions were offered for his name. The family finally decided on Oceanus. Later, when the Mayflower was docked at Cape Cod, a baby was born to the White family. Some of the children wanted to call him Wandering. His parents decided to call him Peregrine.

Make illustrated baby books, depicting the probable events in the first few weeks of the babies' lives.

START TO SCHOOL COLONIAL STYLE

There were few books in colonial American schools. Very young children started their formal education by using hornbooks. A hornbook was not a book at all, but rather a paddle-shaped piece of wood that had the alphabet and the Lord's Prayer written on it. It got its name because a transparent strip of an animal's horn was placed over the writing to protect it. Colonial women often taught school in their homes, using the hornbooks. Children attended these "dame schools" until they could read and write everything on the hornbook.

MAKE A HORNBOOK

1. Cut a paddle shape from a piece of cardboard.

2. Using a white sheet of paper, print the uppercase and lowercase letters. Below these print the Lord's Prayer. Glue this sheet to the front of the paddle.

3. On another sheet of white paper, write some moral sayings for the children to learn. These could be selected proverbs, or sayings of Jesus.
   "My son, hear the instruction of thy father, and forsake not the law of thy mother."
   "A wise man will hear and will increase learning."
   "Knowledge is pleasant unto thy soul."
   "Trust in the Lord with all thine heart."
   "Keep thy heart with all diligence."
   "Even a child is known by his doings."

4. Cover both sides of the hornbook with clear adhesive vinyl.

HAVE AN OLD-TIME SCHOOL DAY

Plan a day to simulate an old-time school. The day will be marked by the absence of many of the routines we consider normal. For example, there would be no flag salute and no hot lunch count during the opening exercises. The children should bring their lunches, preferably in lard buckets—no fancy lunch pails or paper bags. Sandwiches should not be wrapped in waxed paper or plastic wrap, just covered with a cloth. No one may include a soft drink in a lunch, as these had not yet been invented. Milk will be permitted.

For opening exercises the teacher would read from the Bible and pray. The children would join her in singing an old hymn. A moral lesson would be written on the board for the children to learn. This one was used:

In all that you do,
Do with your might.
Things done in halves
Are never done right.

Bibles and religious books were used in the early schools, with much of a day's lessons centering around the Bible. Most of the learning took place by oral recitation. The teacher should state the lesson and the children should repeat it after her. Memory work should be stressed all day long.

Hold a spelling bee. However, accurate spelling was not always considered important in the earliest schools.

Anyone who does not learn the lessons for the day should be placed in a corner with a dunce hat.

Children should work as partners, helping one another with the lessons for the day.

Lunchtime should be taken outside, with the children eating their lunches while sitting on the lawn. Play old-time games, such as tag, ring-around-the-rosy, and go-in-and-out-the-windows.

SCHOOL RULES

RULES FOR CHILDREN

Colonial children had many rules to follow. These rules came from a school in Pennsylvania:

1. Tell no untruths or miscall one another nor use corrupt or unscriptural language.
2. Mind to have your hands and face washed and heads combed every morning before you come to school and be careful to be there by the time appointed.
3. Come into school quietly and soberly. Mind the instructions of the teacher.
4. Move not from seat to seat.
5. Go not outside when it is not necessary.
6. Scribble not in your own book or that of another.
7. Let there be no quarrels, fighting or wrestling in or out of school.
8. Let no one throw dirt, sticks, stones or snowballs.

Compare these rules with the ones children and teachers have to follow today. Make a list of the present rules. Place them in a time capsule to be opened in 25 years.

RULES FOR TEACHERS

This list of rules was taken from a list of requirements dated 1872.

1. Teachers will each day fill lamp and clean the chimney.
2. Each teacher will bring a bucket of water and a shuttle of coal for each day's session.
3. After ten hours in school, teachers may spend the remaining time reading the Bible or other good books.
4. Women teachers who marry will be dismissed.
5. Any teacher who smokes, uses liquor in any form, frequents pool or public halls or gets shaved in a barber shop will give some good reason to suspect his worth, intention and honesty.
6. The teacher who performs his labors faithfully for five years will be given an increase of twenty-five cents per week in his pay, providing the Board of Education approves.

PLAYTIME IN THE COLONIES

Work occupied a large share of colonial children's time, but there was always a little time for fun. The following instructions for a game were taken from a book published during the 1700s, called *The Pretty Little Pocket Book*.

CHUCK-FARTHING

As you value your Pence
At the Hole take your Aim
Chuck all safely in
And You'll win the game.

The games in this book had morals attached to them. The moral for this game was

Chuck-Farthing like Trade
Requires great Care
The more you observe
The better you fare.

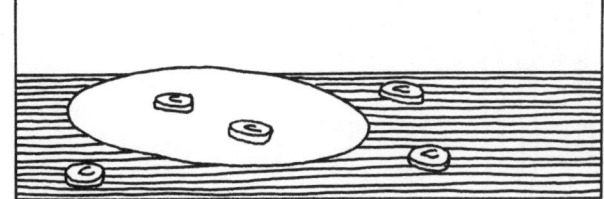

Give each player ten pennies or similar objects. Place a large paper plate in the middle of the playing area. The players try to throw one of their pennies into the plate. The player who comes closest gets to play first. He throws all of his pennies toward the plate. The ones that stay in the plate may be kept by the player. The ones outside the plate are forfeited. The other players then throw their pennies in turn. The game is over when there are no more pennies to throw. The player who was last to keep a penny is the winner.

HOOP ROLLING WAS POPULAR

At the start of this game, all the players lined up at the starting line. At the signal the children used a stick to roll the hoop to the finish line. The first child across the line was the winner. Hula-Hoops can be used to play this game.

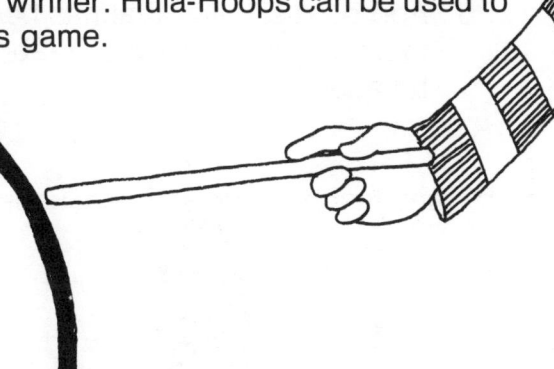

CHILDREN LOVED SINGING GAMES

Many colonial singing games are still played today:
"I Put My Right Foot In," "London Bridge Is Falling Down," "Little Sally Waters," "Here We Go Around the Mulberry Bush."

Play some of these old-time games.

A word of caution: Many activities were not tolerated. Massachusetts Bay Colony passed a law against coasting down snow-covered hills for fun. In the summertime, swimming was not permitted. Both of these activities were considered a waste of time.

CORNHUSK DOLLS

Colonial children had to be content with homemade toys. One popular item was the cornhusk doll. These dolls were originally made by the Indians. The cornhusks were usually dried. Before they were used, they were soaked in water for about 15 minutes to make them pliable. Make a cornhusk doll.

1. Tear husks into narrow strips and roll one husk for the head and another wider one, about 1¼", for the body.

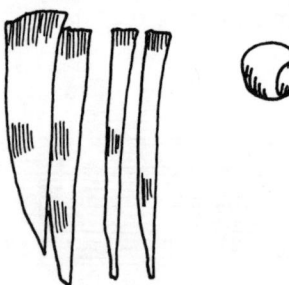

2. Take a long, smooth piece of husk and drape it over the head section, allowing the excess to hang down, adding an outer layer to the body.

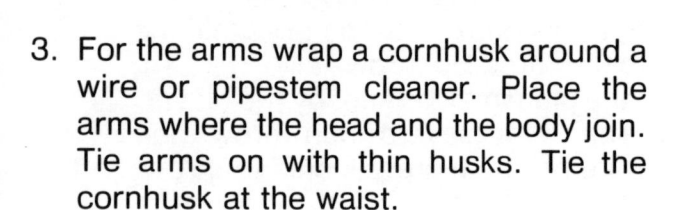

3. For the arms wrap a cornhusk around a wire or pipestem cleaner. Place the arms where the head and the body join. Tie arms on with thin husks. Tie the cornhusk at the waist.

4. Make a skirt by gathering several full cornhusks around the waist. Tie these in place with a thin husk. Trim evenly a little above the waist and along the bottom.

5. Make a blouse by draping a cornhusk over the front and back top section, cutting a hole for the head. Tie neatly at the waist. Bend the arms so they extend downward. Paint on a face.

6. Add corn-silk hair that has been soaked to make it easier to use. A fabric hat may be added.

WHAT'S COOKING IN THE COLONIAL KITCHEN

Pease porridge hot,
Pease porridge cold,
Pease porridge in the pot,
Nine days old.

Some like it hot,
Some like it cold,
Some like it in the pot,
Nine days old.

To our ears this is a nursery rhyme. To the colonial family, it was a description of the family dinner. Often a huge pot of soup was made and left in the back of the fireplace. The family helped themselves when they were hungry. Some thought the soup got better as it simmered for days in the fireplace. See if you agree with them. Make some pease porridge in the classroom, using a modern Crockpot.

PEASE PORRIDGE

2 cups split peas
3 quarts water
2 tsp. salt
2 medium onions
3 stalks celery
2 tsp. dried mint

Place split peas in the 3 qts. of water. Soak overnight in a Crockpot. In the morning add salt and bring the mixture to a boil with the Crockpot on high. Cook for about five minutes. Reduce the heat to low. Simmer for about 3 hours. Finely dice the onions and celery. Add these to the soup. Season with the dried mint. Cook an additional 30 minutes or until the vegetables are tender. Enjoy your pease porridge!

JOHNNYCAKES TO EAT WITH YOUR PORRIDGE

2 cups water
2 cups yellow cornmeal
1 cup milk
1 tsp. salt

Pour the water into a saucepan and bring to a boil. Add the salt. Slowly stir in the cornmeal. Stir until no lumps remain. Add milk. Stir until smooth.

Place two tablespoons of shortening in an electric frying pan. Set on medium heat. Drop spoonfuls of the cornmeal into the pan. Cook until brown. Turn carefully. Brown the other side. Serve with the porridge.

CHANGING KITCHEN TOOLS

When we visit historical museums, we see kitchen artifacts of yesteryear. Often the items have descriptions beside them to tell us how the objects were used. Even in our lifetimes we can see major developments that make our lives easier in the kitchen.

MAKE A KITCHEN DICTIONARY

Imagine colonial children walking into a modern kitchen. How many of the items would they be unable to identify? Make up a kitchen dictionary for the colonial children. Tell how each item is used. Include pictures cut from catalogs to make your dictionary more helpful and colorful.

FOR EXAMPLE
Freezer—Large box used to keep food frozen. Can store supplies for long periods of time.

Toaster—Machine used to brown bread and make it crunchy.

OTHER ITEMS TO INCLUDE
refrigerator, stove, microwave oven, electric fry pan, popcorn popper, waffle iron, pasta maker, food processor, blender, trash compacter, garbage disposal, dishwasher and mixer.

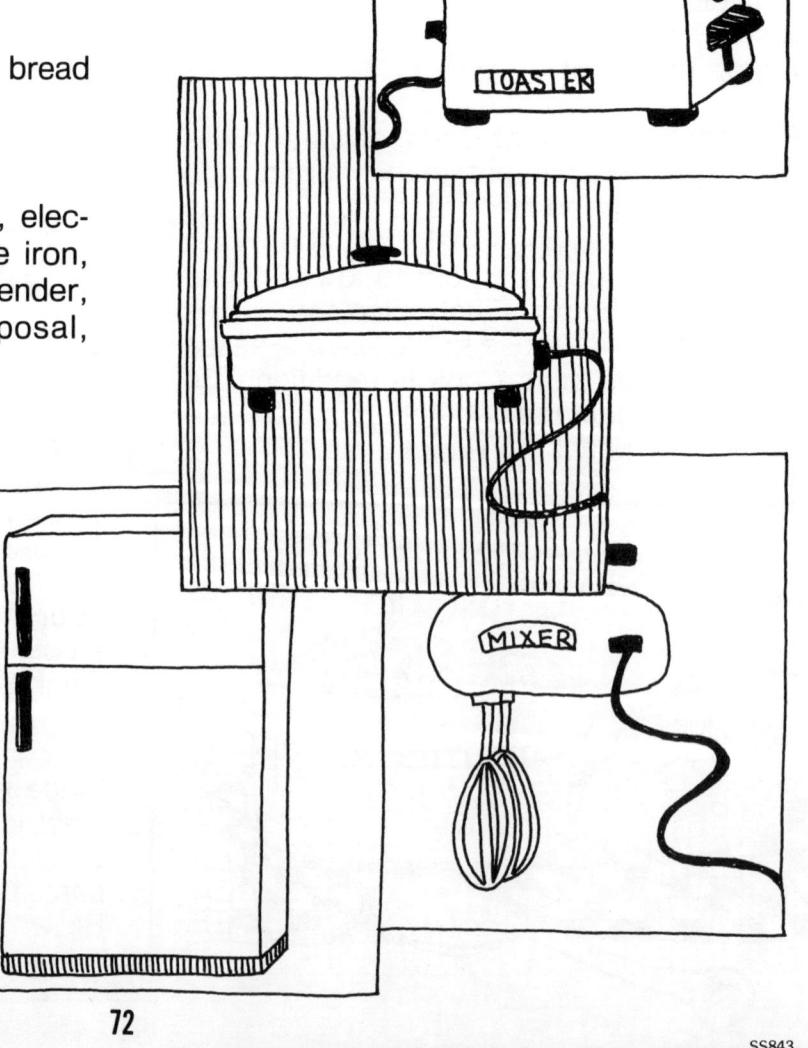

RELIGION IN THE COLONIES

The church strongly influenced social and political life in colonial times. Most of the colonists were deeply religious. Many had come to the new country for religious freedom. However, some were not willing to extend religious freedom to others. The Puritans established the Congregational Church. They denied citizenship to Quakers or others who had a different form of worship. They all had strict rules about how the Sabbath should be observed. One set of rules was called the blue laws.

BLUE LAWS

These laws were first published in New Haven, Connecticut. They were called blue laws because they were bound in blue paper. They seem very odd to us today.

1. No one shall travel, cook, make beds, sweep the house, cut hair or shave on the Sabbath day.
2. No one shall cross a river on the Sabbath except an authorized clergyman.
3. No woman shall kiss her child on the Sabbath or a fasting day.
4. No one shall read common prayer, keep Christmas, make any mince pies, or make any trip except to church.

Have the children make laws that they think would be good for people to use today to keep the Lord's day a special day.

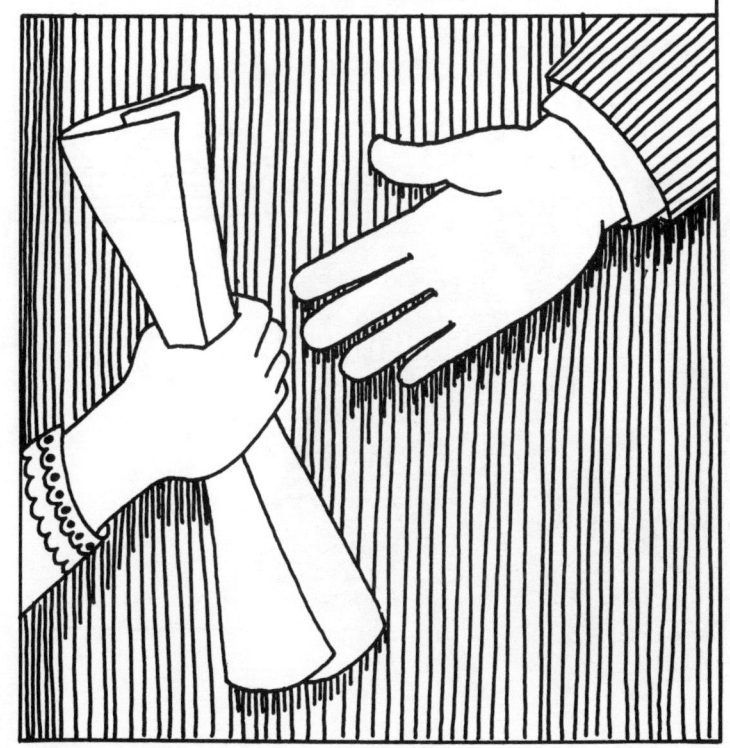

GUIDELINES FOR MINISTERS

Ministers had to be extra good and follow a special set of rules. One church had these rules for its ministers:

> Ministers shall not drink in excess or riot.
> They shall not be idle during the day or night.
> They shall never play dice, cards, or any unlawful game.
> In their free time they should read and study the Holy Scriptures.
> They should always do what is honest and bring glory to the church of God.
> They should be an example to the people and be purer than the other people.

Have the children write guidelines for the present minister. Give these to him.

PILGRIMS
Words by Helen Kitchell Evans
Music by Frances Mann Benson

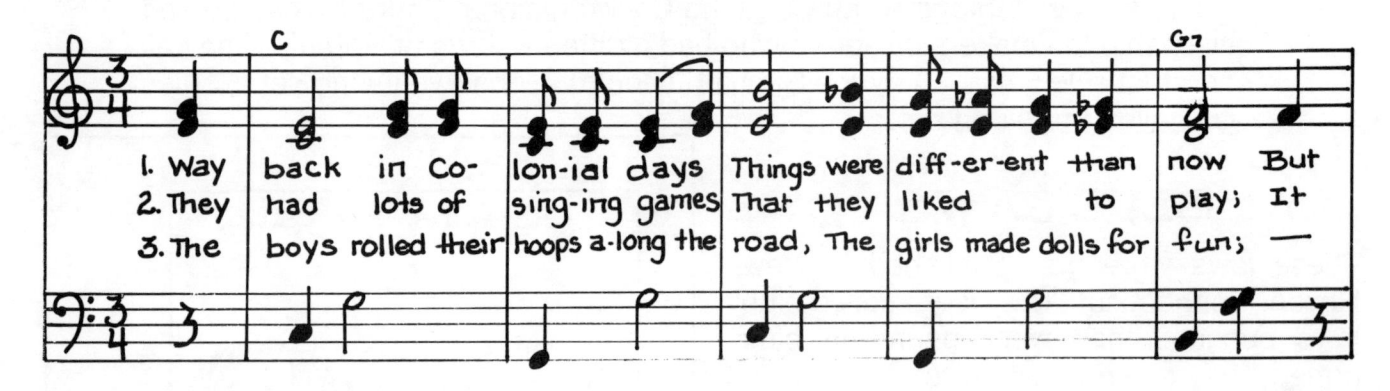

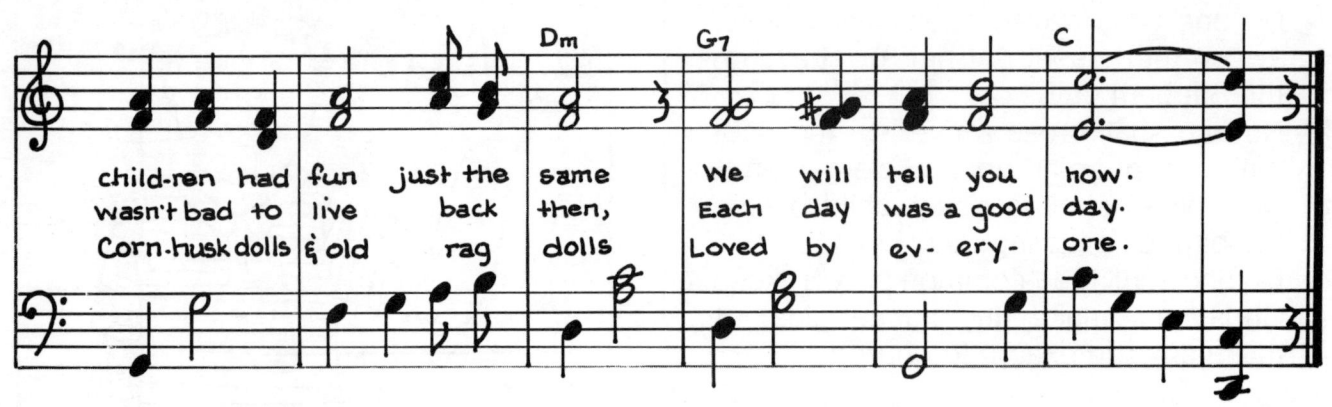

1. Way back in Co-lon-ial days Things were dif-fer-ent than now But child-ren had fun just the same We will tell you how.
2. They had lots of sing-ing games That they liked to play; It wasn't bad to live back then, Each day was a good day.
3. The boys rolled their hoops a-long the road, The girls made dolls for fun; Corn-husk dolls & old rag dolls Loved by ev-ery-one.

A Thoroughfare for Freedom
Beat Across the Wilderness

Bulletin Board Idea

OPENING THE WEST

LEWIS AND CLARK

COWBOYS

PIONEERS

CIRCUIT RIDER

FORTY-NINERS

MARCUS WHITMAN

Cover the bulletin board with light blue butcher paper. Divide it into sections with one-inch black butcher paper. Enlarge the figures shown, or use illustrations done by the children.

Use the board as a motivational tool when introducing the section on the westward movement.

THE WESTWARD TREK
THE PRAIRIE SCHOONER

As pioneers contemplated their westward expedition, their thoughts centered on dependable prairie schooners. Into these vehicles they had to load all of their essential possessions and supplies to insure the success of their adventure. Prairie schooners came in all sizes, but one item all of them had in common was a canvas wagon cover. This was stretched tightly over the wooden bows to protect the contents of the wagon. When people looked at the covered wagons from a distance, they looked like small white ships swaying back and forth. Because of their resemblance to ships, they acquired the name "prairie schooners." Read *The Prairie Schooners* by Glen Rounds. Make a prairie schooner, following the directions on the next page.

PRAIRIE SCHOONER MURAL

Using the information in *The Prairie Schooners*, make a mural depicting a long line of prairie schooners going across the land.

MAKE A PRAIRIE SCHOONER

Cut a half-gallon milk carton in two, lengthwise. Cover one section with wood-grained adhesive paper. Punch 5 equally-spaced holes along both sides, about ½" down from the top.

Cut 5 pieces of wire. Shape these into the wagon's "ribs," resembling croquet wickets, and fasten in each hole.

Cut a piece of muslin long enough to cover the wire frame of the wagon. Add extra fabric to allow for hemming the sides and both ends. Hem the side edges. The ends should then be sewn. Slip a string through the hem on the ends so the opening can be drawn tight.

Sew heavy string to the sides of the muslin at the points where the holes are punched in the milk carton. To attach the cover to the base, slip the string through the holes and tie on the inside of the carton. Draw the string tight on the opening in each end.

Make cardboard wheels and glue them to the sides of the wagon.

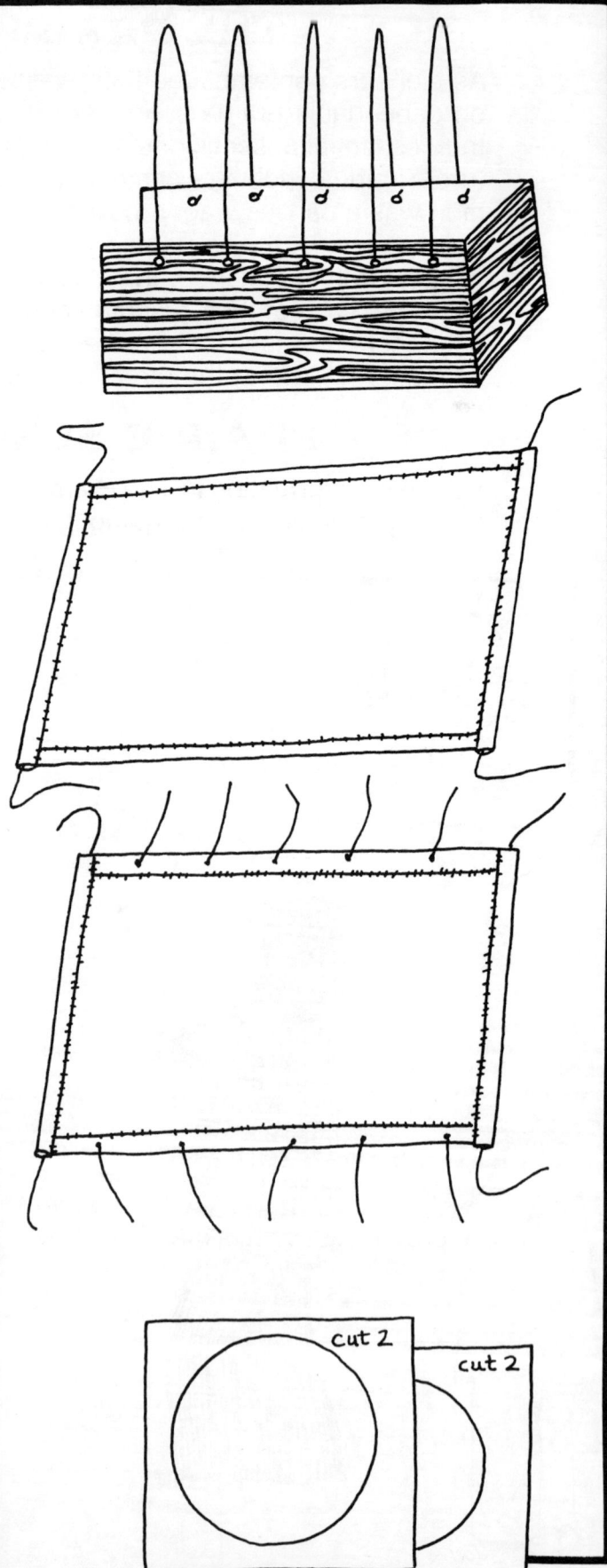

cut 2
cut 2

THE WESTERN COWBOYS

In the days of the western frontier, American cowboys gained fame for the long cattle drives and the dangerous lives they led. Many of the cowboys worked on ranches from Texas to Montana. When the cattle were ready to sell, the cowboys had to drive them to railroad towns so they could be shipped to eastern markets. Cattle drives were long and dangerous, and cowboys had to be strong and well-equipped to survive.

THE COWBOY'S CLOTHING

A cowboy wore tight pants so no loose hanging cloth could catch on plants or trees and pull him from his horse. He usually wore Levi's.

Chaps were made of leather to keep sharp thorns or twigs from tearing his pants. His broad-brimmed hat was designed to keep the sun and wind out of his eyes. The brim was wide enough to catch rainwater for the cowboy to drink. The hat could also be used as a bucket in an emergency.

High-heeled shoes kept his feet from slipping from the stirrups. The high sides protected his legs and provided warmth.

A bandanna could be placed over the cowboy's face to protect his lungs against dust. This was especially important during a stampede, when the cattle were raising a lot of dust.

DESIGN A BANDANNA

Give each child an 18" square of white cotton. Using crayons, have him make cowboy pictures on the cloth. When the art work is finished, lay a strip of waxed paper over the bandanna. Press it with a hot iron to seal the designs.

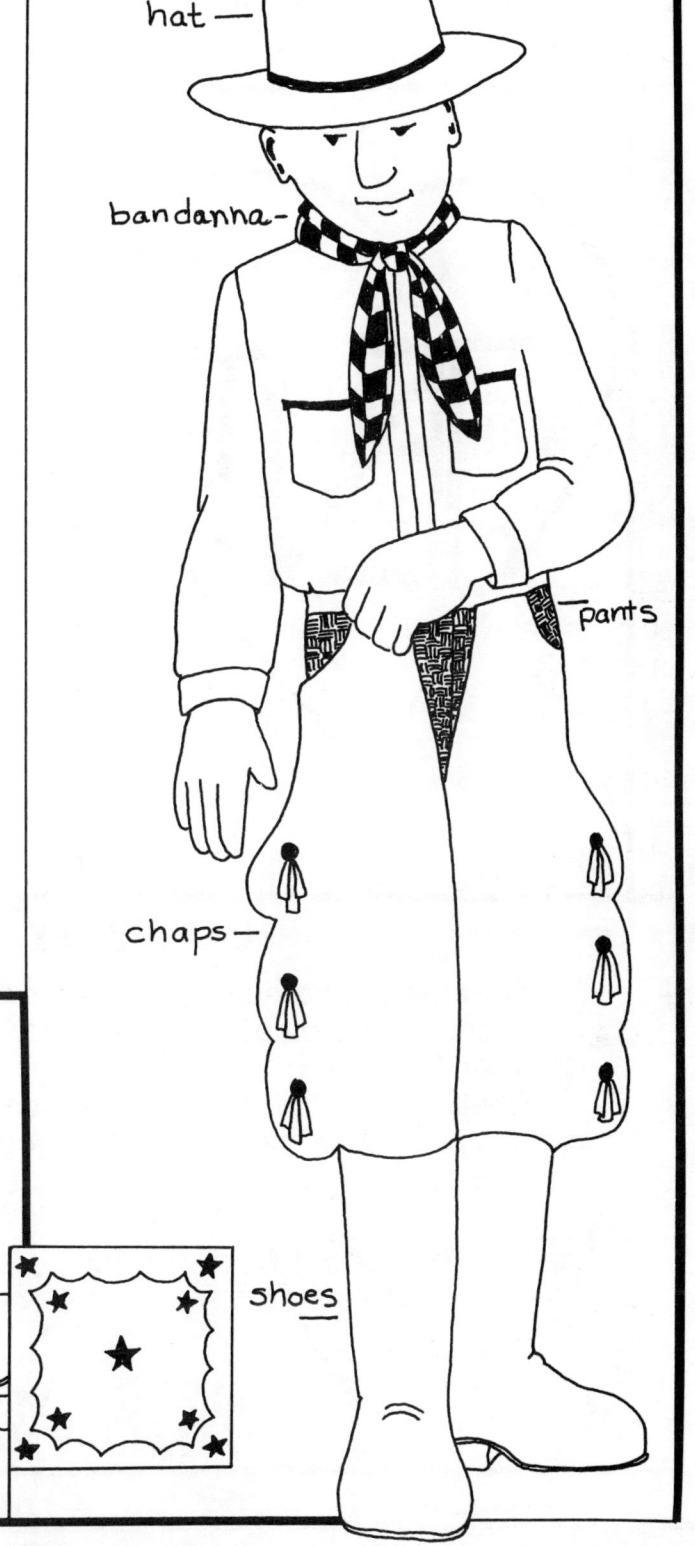

BRANDING CATTLE

Ranchers brand their cattle to identify them if they are lost or stolen. Cattlemen register their brands with the state so no confusion can arise. Everyone has to have an original design; no two brands are alike. This way the cattlemen can positively identify their brands. Design your own cattle brand. Use your name in some way in your brand.

JESUS PLACES A BRAND ON HIS CHILDREN

When children believe in Jesus, He places His holy brand or seal on them. "In whom ye also trusted, after that ye heard the word of truth, the gospel of your salvation: in whom also after that ye believed, ye were sealed with that holy Spirit of promise." (Ephesians 1:13.) Design a seal that Jesus could use to identify you as one of His children. Use one of the good qualities that Jesus might see in children.

COWBOY WORDS

Cowboys have a vocabulary all their own. Make a pictorial dictionary of as many cowboy words as possible. Each child may select one word, write a definition for the word and draw a picture. The pages then should be placed in alphabetical order to form a booklet. Some words to give you a start are *bronco, chaps, corral, chuck wagon, dogie, maverick, muley, lasso, lariat, mustang, shindig, Stetson, tenderfoot,* and *bandanna*.

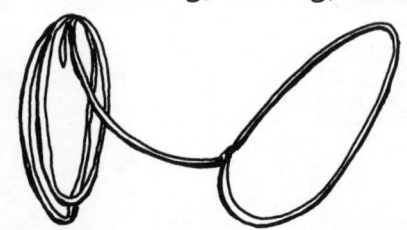

BY ANY OTHER NAME

Cowboys were known by different names. They were called **cowpokes** or **cowpunchers**, because they used sharp sticks to poke the cattle to get them to go into the cattle cars when they were being loaded onto the railroad cars.

Wranglers and **cowhands** were cowboys who tended to the cattle on a ranch.

Other names for cowboys included **buckaroos** and **vaqueros.**

Regardless of the names used for these men, they all took care of cattle, either on ranches or on the long cattle drives.

Jesus has many names too. See which child can make the longest list of names given to Jesus. Examples could include *Prince of Peace, Christ, Savior, Wonderful, Son of God, Bread of Life . . . .*

THE COWBOY'S ROPE

A cowboy's rope was made of horsehair, grass or henequen and was a very important part of his equipment. He tied a honda knot at one end of the rope. The cowboy then passed the other end of the rope through this knot to form a loop. He could pull the rope tight when it was necessary, or he could allow it to go slack, depending on his needs at the moment. Learn to tie a honda knot.

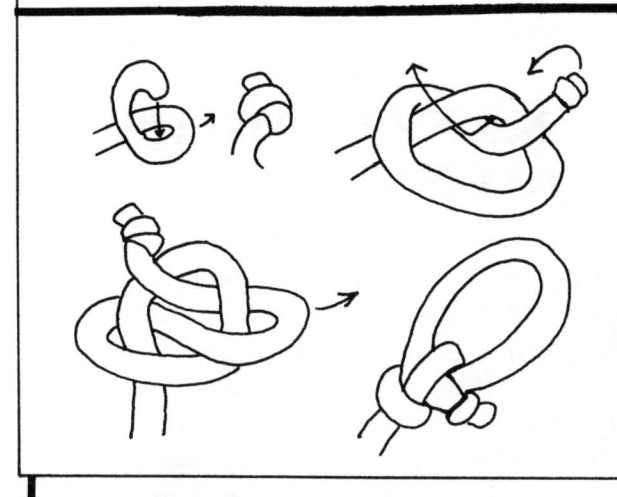

LEWIS AND CLARK EXPEDITION

President Thomas Jefferson needed someone to explore the unknown western lands of North America. His secretary, Meriwether Lewis, had long dreamed of exploring this region, and President Jefferson knew he would be the perfect one for the job. Lewis chose his friend William Clark to accompany him on the expedition. On May 14, 1804, the party of men began their trek westward. President Jefferson hoped they would find a navigable water route to the west. However, the explorers discovered that no such route existed. Many difficult weeks and months passed before the brave crew reached the Pacific Ocean.

MANY DANGERS ALONG THE WAY

The explorers encountered many dangers along the way. They met hostile Indians who tried to steal their equipment and endangered their lives. The terrain was difficult, and they sometimes wondered how they could climb the high mountains and carry their equipment overland. The weather was sometimes severe. Read *Lewis and Clark*, by Elizabeth Rider Montgomery, to the children.

GOOD FORTUNE ALONG THE WAY

While the explorers often had a hard time, they also experienced much good fortune. Sacagawea, an Indian girl, joined the explorers. Her knowledge of the Indian people and the land helped them survive in almost impossible situations. Some of the Indians were friendly and helped them by guiding the explorers through their territory and advising them on the best routes.

CONSTRUCT A DIORAMA

Have each child select a different phase of this exciting expedition and construct a diorama. Place each diorama in a line in the correct time order, so a panoramic view of the entire trip can be seen.

THE CIRCUIT RIDER

As families moved west, they were very busy clearing the wilderness, building homes, and trying to make a living. For many years there were few churches. The first ministers to come to the West were the circuit riders. They traveled from one settlement to another on horseback. They usually held their services in the cabins of the pioneers. The circuit rider had a lot of territory to cover. He often took many weeks or even months to travel around his circuit. Besides preaching, the circuit rider brought news to the pioneers. He also conducted marriages and baptisms. In order to carry out all his obligations, the circuit rider usually kept a very accurate journal.

A CLASS JOURNAL

Start a classroom journal. Make daily entries concerning the class or the personal happenings in the lives of the students.

Jan. 3 Jason's little brother was born today.
Jan. 4 Linda's sister got married.
Jan. 5 Our class went to the museum.

CAMP MEETINGS

When the weather was favorable, the circuit rider would hold camp meetings for all the people in his districts. The purpose of the camp meeting was to renew the spiritual lives of his people. In addition, this was often a social occasion, as families would bring food and stay for long weekends. When they were not attending the meetings, the pioneers could visit with new friends.

Since communication was not very advanced, often the circuit rider would have handbills published and pass them out in the community so everyone would know when a camp meeting was to be held.

MAKE A HANDBILL

Make handbills to advertise a camp meeting to be held soon in your area. Include the name of the minister, his sermon topics, the date, the place, and reasons for people to attend.

Come to an Old Fashioned Camp Meeting
For your spiritual renewal.
March 16-20
Boise, Idaho
Rev. Harold Antrene will speak on Spiritual Gifts.

Bring the whole family and enjoy a week of fellowship.

MISSIONARIES TO OREGON

". . . all power is given unto me in heaven and In earth. Go ye therefore, and teach all nations, baptizing them in the name of the Father, and of the Son, and of the Holy Ghost: Teaching them to observe all things whatsoever I have commanded you: and, lo, I am with you always, even unto the end of the world. Amen." Matthew 28:18-20

To Dr. Marcus and Narcissa Whitman this command of Jesus meant for them to go to the Indians in the Oregon country. They joined two other missionaries, Henry and Eliza Spaulding, who were also going to Oregon. Because it was not safe to travel alone, they went with a fur trading company. The trail was extremely dangerous. Narcissa and Eliza persevered, however, and they became the first two white women to cross the Rocky Mountains. The Whitmans' mission was to the Cayuse Indians. These people were very difficult to convert. The Whitmans labored faithfully, trying to help the Indians with their farming and their medical needs, but their efforts were not always appreciated.

The Cayuse Indians killed the Whitmans because some white families infected Indian children with measles. Though they no longer lived, the memory of the missionaries lived on and encouraged more families to travel the Oregon Trail to set up homes in the West. Learn the missionary Bible verses from Matthew 28:18-20.

GO AND TEACH ALL NATIONS

_____

has learned Matthew 28:18-20.

_____

date

_____

teacher

THE GOLD RUSH

On January 24, 1848, James Wilson Marshall found gold at Sutter's Mill in California. By 1849 the gold rush was in full bloom. Miners came from all parts of the country. Stagecoaches, guides, and sea captains all enjoyed a thriving business as thousands flocked to California. A few people did strike it rich, but the cost of supplies was so outlandish that many prospectors were able to provide for only their basic needs.

DRAW A PICTURE

From Genesis to Revelation, gold has been important to man. In Revelation 21:18-21 a description is given of the golden streets in heaven. No gold rush will take place, because the gold will be so plentiful. Using this Scripture, draw pictures of what heaven might look like. Display the pictures on the bulletin board.

SOD HOUSES

When pioneers pushed westward to the plains, they discovered that there were no trees available to build cabins, so farmers built their houses from sod. The men cut squares about one foot thick and piled the blocks on top of one another. When the walls were erected, roofs of thatch completed the structures. The sod often crumbled and made the inside of the houses dirty. Sometimes the farmers whitewashed the structures to preserve them.

MAKE A SOD HOUSE

Make a sod house. Using brown clay, cut one-inch squares. Stack them to form the walls. Place a brown construction-paper roof over the walls. Glue narrow strips of yellow construction paper on the roof to resemble thatch. Fill in the roof completely.

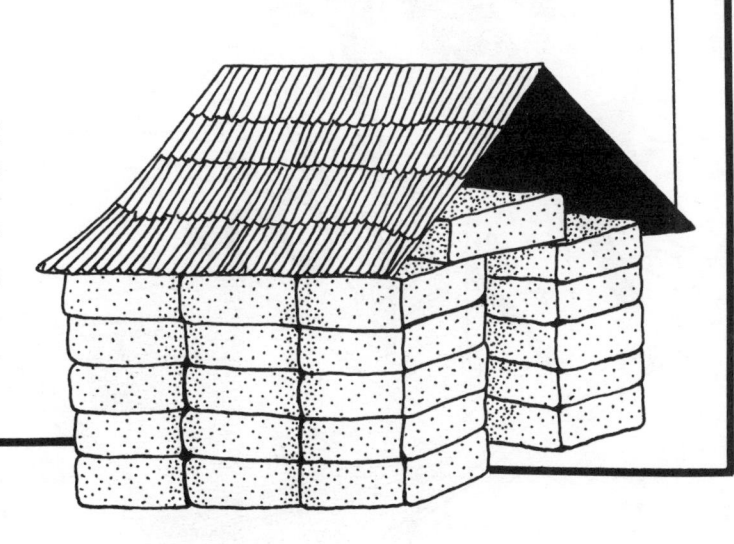

THE OVERLAND STAGE

As settlers moved west, transportation had to be provided. The Concord overland stagecoaches were right for the times. They were built sturdily to withstand the rough terrain over which they traveled. The overland stagecoaches were about eight feet high and weighed about a ton. Most of the stagecoaches were beautifully handcrafted and were equipped luxuriously. The selling price was from $625 to $1120.

Write a newspaper advertisement offering one of these stagecoaches for sale.

WATCH THE BAGGAGE LIMIT

Passengers on the stage were limited to twenty-five pounds of baggage each. In order to transport all of their necessities, they often wore several layers of clothing. In addition, they filled their pockets to the brim with small items.

Weigh twenty-five pounds of items to show what a small amount this really was, especially since the travelers had to take all their own supplies for the trip.

Decide what the children would place in their own pockets if they were to take a trip on the stagecoach.

For the utmost in comfort, test drive one of our luxurious coaches. Priced to please. Only $795.00

STRONG HORSES PULL THE COACHES

Horses pulled the stagecoaches for about ten to twenty miles a day. Then another team was hitched to take the stagecoach on the next leg of its journey. It took horses about twenty days to go from Kansas to California.

THE RAILROAD CHANGES THE WEST

When the railroad came to the West, a dramatic change was evident. People could move to the West easily. Supplies could be obtained from the East more quickly and safely. New towns were built all along the route.

The race to connect the East to the West was a dramatic one. The Central Pacific Railroad started at Sacramento, California. It was to lay tracks eastward. The Union Pacific Railroad started at Omaha, Nebraska. It was to lay tracks westward. Daily newspaper reports kept Americans informed about the progress of the railroad companies. It seemed as if the whole country was cheering them on to completion. Rivalries were evident as each company tried to lay more track in one day than the other company. Finally, on May 10, 1869, a golden spike was pounded into the last rail to symbolize the joining of the East to the West.

MAKE RAILROAD CARS

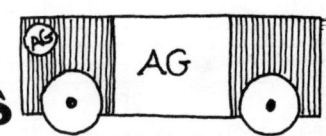

Shoe boxes make good cars. Cover the boxes with gray or red adhesive paper.

Make cardboard wheels. Attach the wheels with brass fasteners, keeping them loose enough so the wheels can move.

Make a hole in the front and back of each box. Slip a heavy cord through the holes. Tie a knot just inside each end of the box to keep the cord from sliding through the box after it is finished.

To make the engine, turn a shoe box upside down. Cover it with black adhesive paper. Cover a Pringle's potato chip can with black adhesive paper, and glue it to the shoe box.

On the top of the engine, attach a cardboard bell which has been covered with aluminum foil. Make a cowcatcher by folding aluminum foil in accordian pleats. Glue this to the front of the engine.

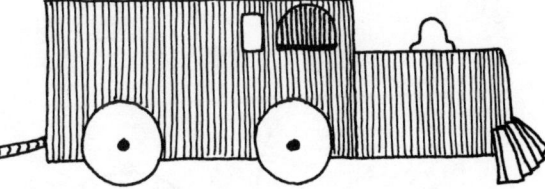

A PART OF HISTORY

Words by Helen Kitchell Evans
Music by Frances Mann Benson

1. Lewis and Clark explored the west, Others, too, were brave;
2. Cowboys roping cattle Across the western plains, Men
3. That's all part of history Of this great land we love;

We should all be thankful for these men and what they gave.
digging for gold nuggets and farmers raising grain.
Surely God blesses us From Heaven up above.

America! America! God Mend Thine Ev'ry Flaw, Confirm Thy Soul in Self-Control, Thy Liberty in Law.

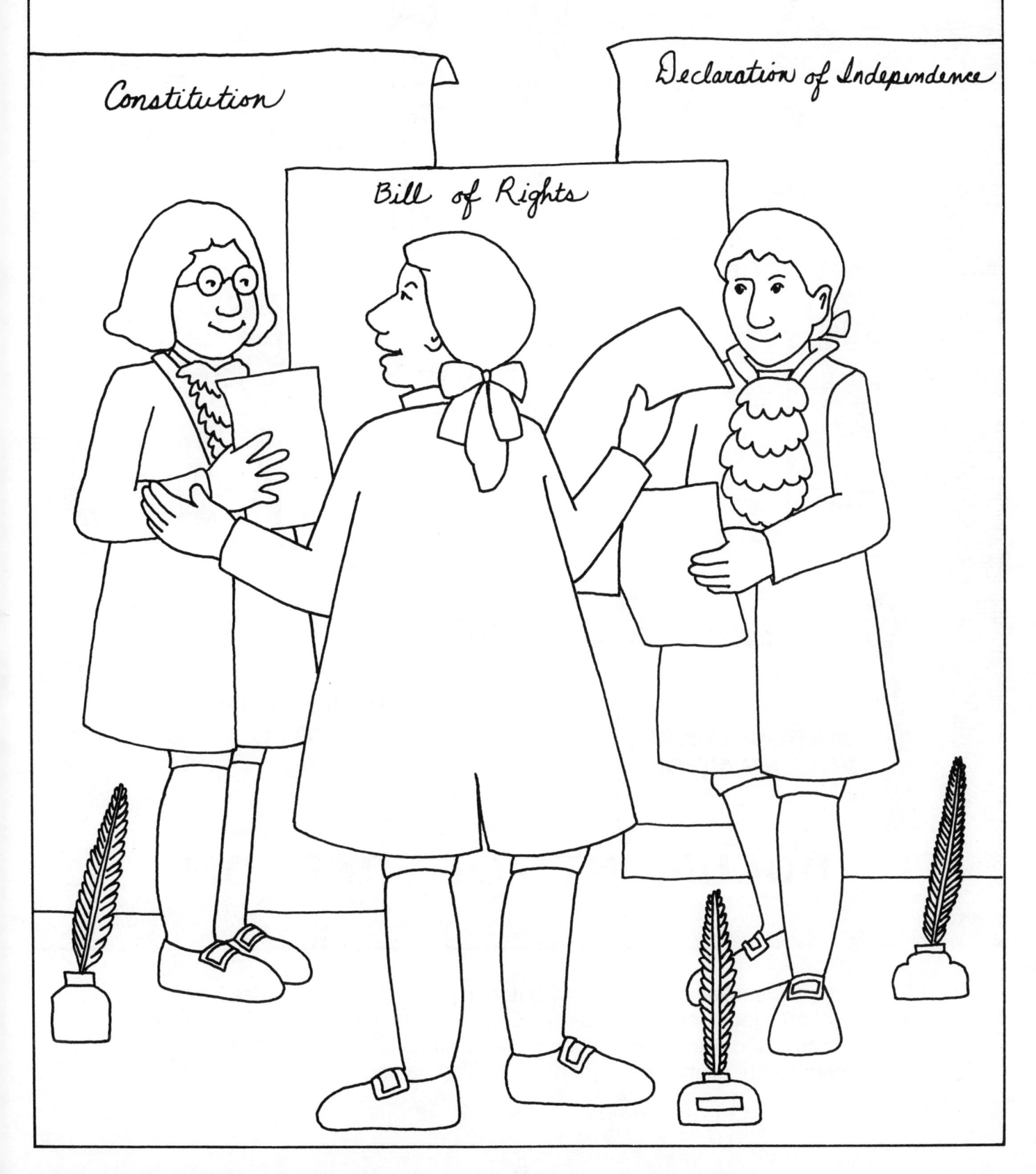

Bulletin Board Idea

MAYFLOWER COMPACT

DECLARATION OF INDEPENDENCE

CONSTITUTION

BILL OF RIGHTS

EMANCIPATION PROCLAMATION

WOMEN'S RIGHT TO VOTE

DOCUMENTS OF FREEDOM

Cover the bulletin board with white butcher paper. Cut the border from red construction paper. Make the letters blue. The documents should be on white paper, mounted on red construction paper. Emphasize one portion of each of these documents every day, right after the flag salute.

MAYFLOWER COMPACT

When the Pilgrims sailed from England on the Mayflower, they were seeking freedom in the new country. They had permission from the London Company to settle in Viriginia, but because of storms they were blown off course and landed in New England. The London Company had no authority there, so responsible leaders of the Mayflower expedition decided to make laws for the people to follow before they went ashore. They made wise decisions to help the people survive. While this document applied to only one small colony, it set an important precedent for others to follow. It demonstrated that the people could make laws and govern themselves responsibly.

MAKE A COMPACT

Help your children make a compact for their home or classroom.

Class compact

Children will be courteous to their teachers and classmates.

DECLARATION OF INDEPENDENCE

The Continental Congress had been meeting in Philadelphia. Many of the representatives were unhappy with the injustices England had imposed on the thirteen colonies. On June 7, 1776, Richard Henry Lee, a delegate from Virginia, stated ". . . these united colonies are and of right ought to be free and independent states."

Many of the representatives agreed. A committee was appointed, and Thomas Jefferson was asked to write the Declaration of Independence. Upon completion of his work, Jefferson's committee made slight changes. It was then adopted by the Continental Congress. The soldiers in the Revolutionary War were fighting not only for their rights, but to found an independent country. The document recognized that our Creator gave us inalienable rights. It also asked for God's protection as the nation sought to obtain these rights.

LEARN A SONG

Learn the song "Great Democracy," on page 94.

CONSTITUTION OF THE UNITED STATES

The Constitution of the United States outlines the plan of government for our country. After the patriots had won the Revolutionary War, our country's leaders asked the states to send delegates to a convention in Philadelphia, where they would draft a constitution for the new nation. George Washington was chosen as President of the convention. The delegates pooled their ideas to make the central government an agency which would serve the people. They decided to have three branches of government. The legislative branch would make laws. The executive branch would carry out the laws, and the judicial branch would interpret the laws. To placate both the large and small states, it was decided to have two legislative bodies. The Senate would have equal representation. The number of members in the House of Representatives would be based on the population of the states. The Constitution was signed on September 17, 1787. George Washington was the first signer of the document. It was later approved by the states. In the Preamble, the purpose of the Constitution is outlined. Learn the Preamble.

☆ PREAMBLE ☆

We the people of the United States, in order to form a more perfect Union, establish justice, insure domestic tranquility, provide for the common defense, promote the general welfare, and secure the blessings of liberty to ourselves and our posterity, do ordain and establish this Constitution for the United States of America.

GOD'S LAWS

When the children of Israel came out of Egypt, God knew that the people of this young nation would need laws to help guide their actions. God gave them the Ten Commandments to help them live godly and productive lives. Memorize the Ten Commandments. (Exodus 20:3-17)

TEN COMMANDMENTS AWARD

This is to certify that

_____

has learned the Ten Commandments

_____

date

_____

signature

BILL OF RIGHTS

The Constitution of the United States outlined how the government should be operated. However, people who valued personal liberty felt that the rights of citizens should be included in the Constitution. The first ten amendments were called the Bill of Rights. Among these rights are freedom of religion, freedom of speech, freedom of the press, right of assembly, right to keep and bear arms, and the right to a trial by jury.

Have the children compose a Bill of Rights for Children.

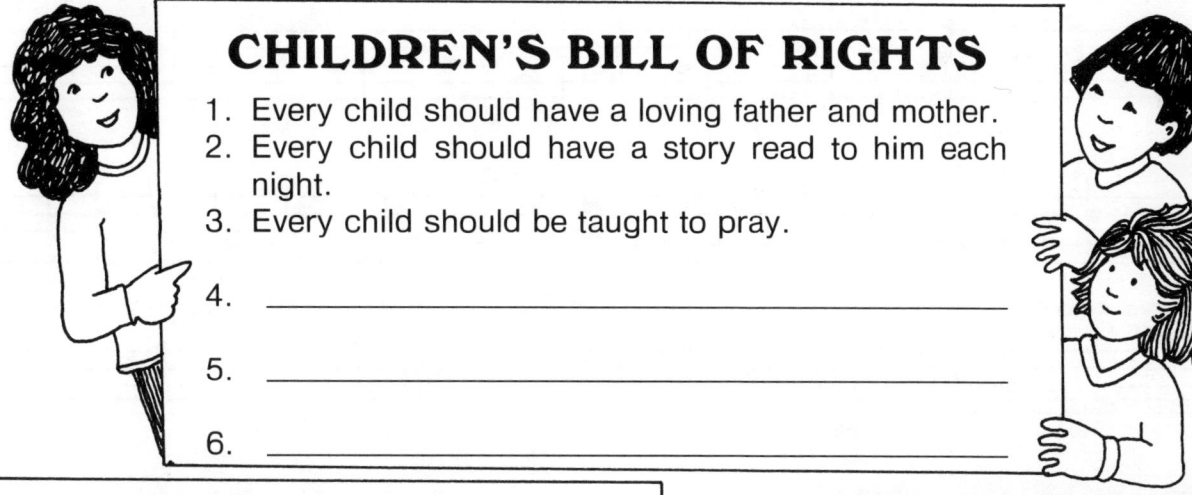

CHILDREN'S BILL OF RIGHTS

1. Every child should have a loving father and mother.
2. Every child should have a story read to him each night.
3. Every child should be taught to pray.
4. _____
5. _____
6. _____

HAVE A MINI DEMOCRACY FAIR

Make small booths from half-gallon milk cartons. Decorate each booth to represent one of our documents or national symbols. Station a child "expert" at each booth. Invite another class to the fair.

THE FREEDOM AMENDMENTS

Other amendments to our Constitution guarantee freedom to individuals. The thirteenth amendment abolished slavery and gave freedom to black people. The fourteenth amendment granted citizenship to the former slaves. It stated that all people born or naturalized in the United States are citizens. The fifteenth amendment gave blacks the right to vote. The nineteenth amendment gave women the right to vote.

God declared many years ago that all people are equal in His eyes.

Learn His verses about freedom and equality.

"For ye are all the children of God by faith in Christ Jesus. For as many of you as have been baptized into Christ have put on Christ. There is neither Jew nor Greek, there is neither bond nor free, there is neither male nor female: for ye are all one in Christ Jesus." Galatians 3:26-28

GREAT DEMOCRACY
Words by Helen Kitchell Evans
Music by Frances Mann Benson

Our founding fathers never could foretell That their great constitution would serve so very well: The Bill of Rights set for you and me Made our great America A great democracy. America, America, loyal will we be; for we are blessed with a great democracy.

O Beautiful for Heroes Prov'd in Liberating Strife, Who More Than Self Their Country Loved, and Mercy More Than Life

Bulletin Board Idea

PEOPLE WITH BRIGHT IDEAS

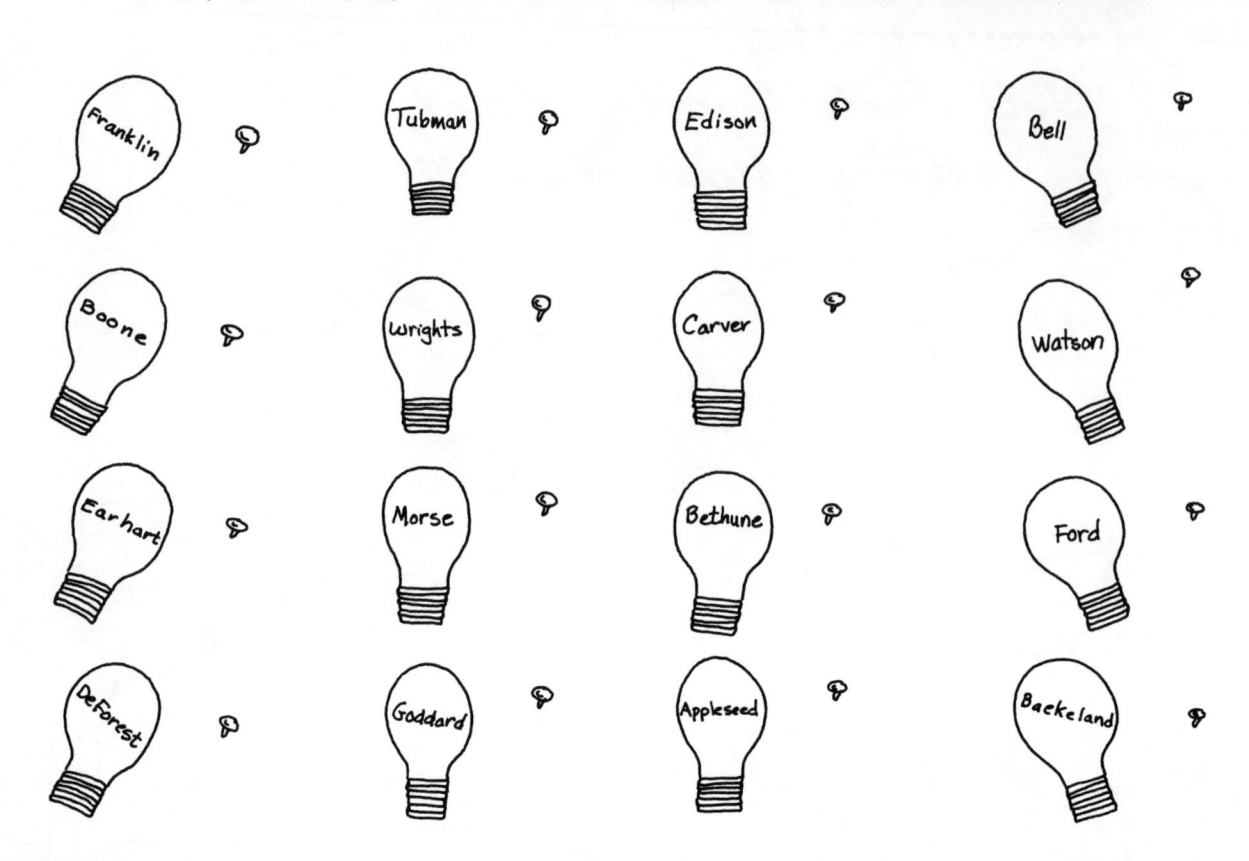

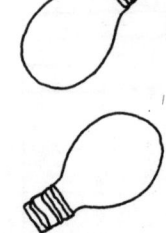

Make sixteen yellow light bulbs and sixteen white light bulbs. On the yellow bulbs write the names listed below. On the white bulbs write the accomplishments of the people. Pin the yellow bulbs on the bulletin board, placing an extra pin beside each. Punch a hole in the top of each white bulb. The children will match the names on the yellow bulbs with the accomplishments of the people on the white bulbs. Slip the white bulbs on the pins next to the correct yellow bulbs.

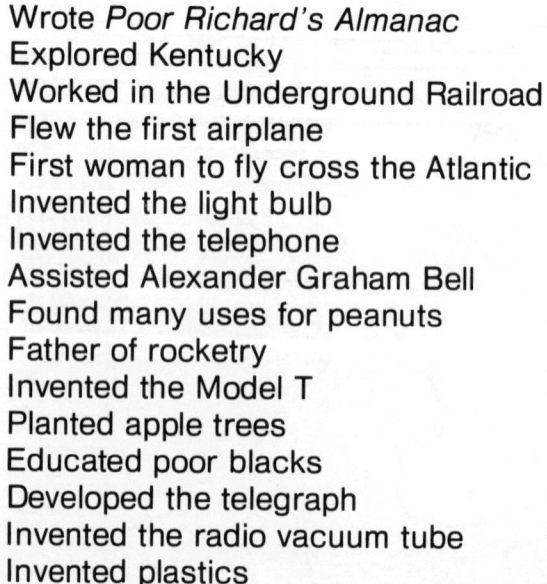

1.	Benjamin Franklin	Wrote *Poor Richard's Almanac*
2.	Daniel Boone	Explored Kentucky
3.	Harriet Tubman	Worked in the Underground Railroad
4.	Wright Brothers	Flew the first airplane
5.	Amelia Earhart	First woman to fly cross the Atlantic
6.	Thomas Edison	Invented the light bulb
7.	Alexander Graham Bell	Invented the telephone
8.	Mr. Watson	Assisted Alexander Graham Bell
9.	George Washington Carver	Found many uses for peanuts
10.	Robert Goddard	Father of rocketry
11.	Henry Ford	Invented the Model T
12.	Johnny Appleseed	Planted apple trees
13.	Mary McLeod Bethune	Educated poor blacks
14.	Samuel Morse	Developed the telegraph
15.	Lee DeForest	Invented the radio vacuum tube
16.	Leo Baekeland	Invented plastics

Shining Star Publications, Copyright © 1987, A division of Good Apple, Inc.

SS843

SALUTE TO BENJAMIN FRANKLIN

Benjamin Franklin served his country as a scientist, an inventor and a statesman. He helped to mold the documents which gave America its guidelines. He signed both the Constitution of the United States and the Declaration of Independence. He was the fifteenth child in a family of seventeen. His parents were godly people who wanted their children to do their very best. Ben went to school for only two years and was good in reading but poor in arithmetic. When his father could no longer afford to send him to school, Ben began to work in the family business, making candles and soap. Ben did not like this kind of work, so he was sent to learn the printing trade from his brother. Later Ben had his own printing shop. He published a very popular annual book called *Poor Richard's Almanac*.

BRAINSTORM

Making soap and candles was too routine for such a creative mind as Franklin possessed. Writing and publishing gave him an outlet for his creativity. Have children think about what is routine in their lives. Brainstorm about how they can change those situations. Franklin changed his world by using the creative gifts God gave him. Ask the children to think about ways they would like to change their world. Remind them that God has given each one a special gift to use.

". . . But every man hath his proper gift of God, one after this manner, and another after that."   I Corinthians 7:7

My talent...

IDENTIFY

Identify special interests and gifts of the children. Discuss how they can use their gifts to change their world.

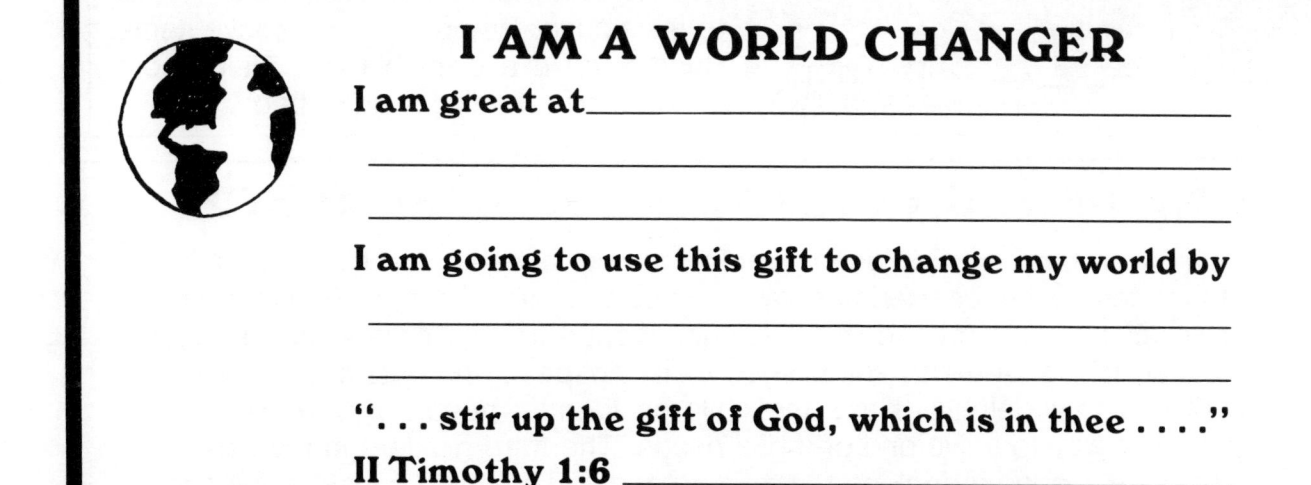

I AM A WORLD CHANGER

I am great at _____
_____
_____

I am going to use this gift to change my world by
_____
_____

". . . stir up the gift of God, which is in thee . . . ."
II Timothy 1:6 _____
Child's signature

MAKE AN ALMANAC

Poor Richard's Almanac was published by Benjamin Franklin from 1733 to 1758. It contained jokes, poems, advice, proverbs, tide tables, witty sayings and weather predictions, among other things.

Have each child make up a page for an almanac. Some sayings of Franklin could be included:

"A penny saved is a penny earned."

"Early to bed, early to rise makes a man healthy, wealthy and wise."

The children may make up their own wise sayings. Include in the almanac reminders of what happened on this day in history, recipes, and good advice for children.

BIG JOE'S ALMANAC

JANUARY 17

Big Joe says,
He who plays hard in the fluffy snow
Will make his muscles and body grow.

1706

On this day in history, the great Benjamin Franklin was born. He invented the Franklin stove and the first bifocal glasses.

Weather prediction:
Expect cloudy, cold weather. Six inches of snow will fall.

RECIPE FOR A COLD DAY

1 pair boots
1 warm scarf
1 heavy coat
1 snug cap
1 pair woolly mittens

Place all the above items on the body in the order listed. Go outdoors in zero-degree weather. Play in the snow one hour. Return to the house. Remove all the above items. Bundle up in a cozy blanket. Relax completely while reading a good book.

ONE PERSON CAN MAKE A DIFFERENCE

In whatever position Benjamin Franklin found himself, he tried to make changes for the better. He improved the postal system and provided for city delivery of mail. He started the first subscription library, organized the first volunteer fire department, established a city hospital, and obtained lights for the city of Philadelphia. Have the children identify needs of your school. Organize a way to solve one of those needs. The third graders in my school decided we needed a drinking fountain outdoors. They held cupcake sales to finance the project. Now everyone in the school can use the fountain on warm days.

PIONEER EXPLORER DANIEL BOONE

Daniel Boone was one of the most famous pioneer explorers. He explored Kentucky and blazed trails for future settlers to follow. He had been raised in a Quaker home, where he was taught that a peaceful life was the ideal one. As a child he had little formal schooling, but he knew how to survive in the wilderness. He learned Indian ways from a friendly tribe that lived near his father's farm. He was later able to use this knowledge to outsmart the Indians at their own tricks. When he was about 20 years old, a man told him about a rich hunting area in the West. Young Daniel could not get the thought of this area out of his mind. One day in 1769 he set out with some friends to find the great land of Kentucky.

When he left home, Daniel Boone wore a fringed hunting shirt, deerskin leggings and moccasins. Later he began to wear his famous coonskin cap. The men soon found a narrow Indian trail that led through the mountains. Boone supervised a group which improved the road. It became known as the Wilderness Road, which led to the West. Many pioneers were grateful for Daniel Boone's ability to blaze a trail for them.

MAKE A COONSKIN CAP

Cut a strip of card stock 2½" wide and long enough to go around the child's head, with a short overlapping edge to staple it. Cut a circle for the top of the hat and glue it in place. Cut a raccoon tail from cardboard, and glue it to the back of the hat. Purchase some fake fur at the fabric store and cover the hat with it.

Quilt batting is a less expensive covering if many caps are to be made, as it may be purchased by the yard. Cut it to the correct size, and glue to the hat. The children may use brushes or sponges to paint their hats.

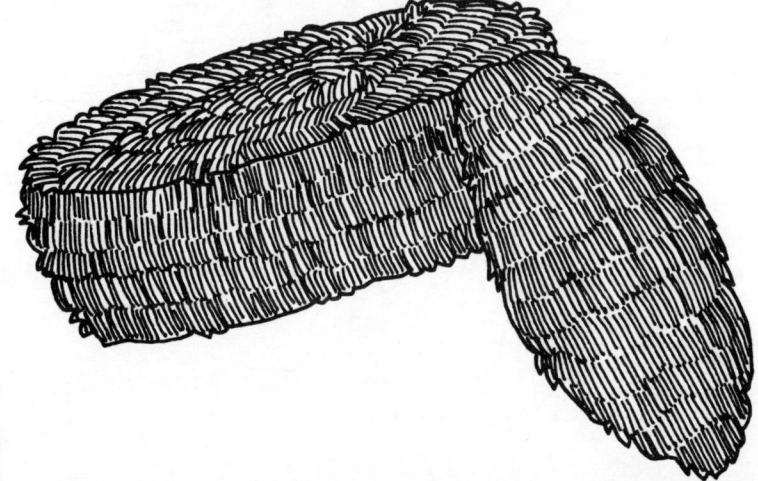

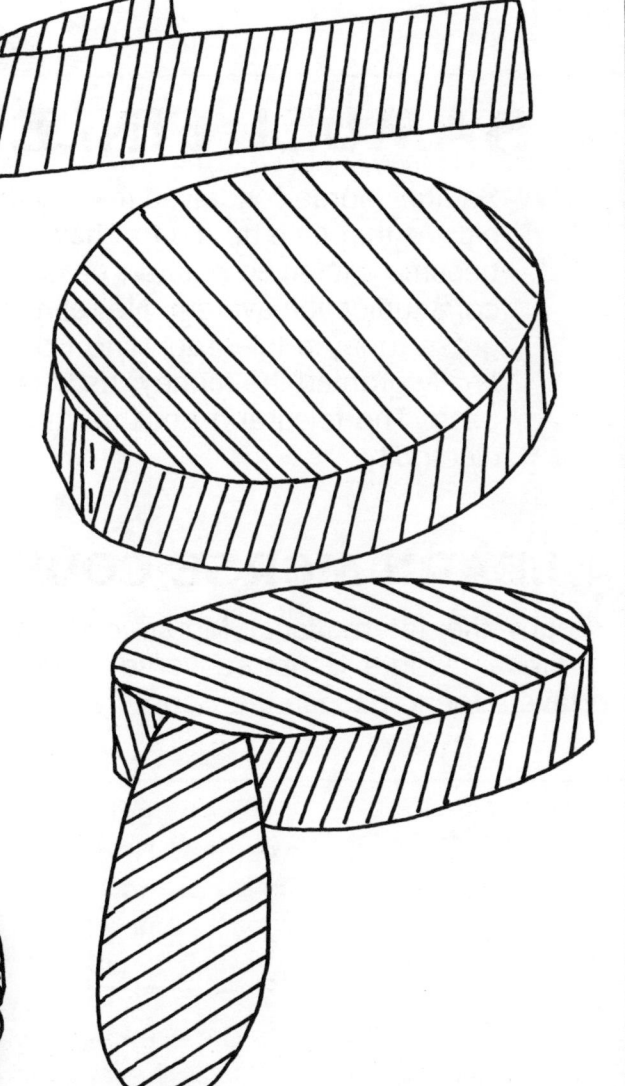

ELI WHITNEY

Eli Whitney's mechanical ability was evident while he was still a youth working on the family farm and in his father's workshop. During the Revolutionary War he started a business making hand-forged nails. Later, he taught school and planned to study law. However, he heard southern farmers discussing the need for a practical cotton gin, and after working for only a short time, he was able to build an effective working model. His machine could do as much work in one day as fifty men. He went into business, but other companies infringed on his patent and built gins without his permission. The cotton gin changed the way Americans lived. They could now have cotton clothing that was inexpensive and easy to obtain.

HAVE A FASHION SHOW

Have the children write a commentary for different articles of cotton clothing. Children should take turns being the commentator and the models for the fashion show.

SAMUEL FINLEY BREESE MORSE

Samuel Morse conceived the idea for the telegraph when he was only 19 years old. At that time he did not have the funds to carry out his idea. Although he became a talented painter, he could not forget his idea of making an effective communication system. He refined his code and tried to get funds from Congress to lay a telegraph line from Baltimore to Washington D.C. When they finally granted the money, he was able to demonstrate his invention with success. The telegraph became the first system of communication operated by electricity.

LEARN MORSE CODE

Learn the International Morse code and write a favorite Scripture verse using it. Have a friend decode the Scripture.

A	·−	M	−−	X	−··−
B	−···	N	−·	Y	−·−−
C	−·−·	O	−−−	Z	−−··
D	−··	P	·−−·		
E	·	Q	−−·−		
F	··−·	R	·−·	?	··−−··
G	−−·	S	···	,	−−··−−
H	····	T	−	.	·−·−·−
I	··	U	··−		
J	·−−−	V	···−		
K	−·−	W	·−−		
L	·−··				

1	·−−−−	6	−····
2	··−−−	7	−−···
3	···−−	8	−−−··
4	····−	9	−−−−·
5	·····	0	−−−−−

MEET JOHNNY APPLESEED

America has many great folk heroes. Some are the products of fertile imaginations; other heroes actually existed. There really was a Johnny Appleseed. He was born Jonathan Chapman in 1774. As a child Johnny loved to study the habits of the wild creatures. He loved the frontier and he loved God. When he was about 25 years old, he began his life's work of reading the Bible to the settlers, planting apple trees and living among the wild creatures. People everywhere loved him for his gentle and loving manner and his helpful ways. The countryside blossomed with the fruit of his work. Use one of Johnny's apples to make an apple-head doll.

APPLE-HEAD DOLL

1. Choose a medium-sized apple. It will shrink one-third its original size.
2. Peel the apple and select its smoothest side.
3. Cut features in the face:
   Make ¼" deep circles for the eyes. Use the points of scissors to carve these. Make a triangular ridge where the nose will be, but do not remove this section. To form the cheeks, use the point of the scissors to hollow out slight indentations beside and under the nose. Make a slash for the mouth, removing very little of the apple from this section.
4. To prevent excessive darkening, dip the apple in lemon juice and salt.
5. To dry, place the head in the oven on the lowest heat. Leave overnight or longer.
6. When the apple is dry, paint the face.

MAKE THE BODY FOR THE DOLL

Make a wire frame for the body, bending it to make a neck, two arms, a body and two legs. Slip the wire into the apple head. Use scraps from old jeans and a red hankerchief or some calico to make pants and a shirt. Stuff cotton inside them to give shape. Make the hands and feet from scraps of felt. Use aluminum foil to make a pan-shaped hat. Paint on the hair, or use fake fur.

BLACKS WHO CHANGED THEIR WORLD

"... I will bless thee ... and thou shalt be a blessing."   Genesis 12:2

MARY MCLEOD BETHUNE

Mary McLeod Bethune was one of seventeen children born of southern black parents. Determined to get an education, she surmounted tremendous obstacles to attain her goal: graduating from high school and later attending Moody Bible Institute. She used her skills with the love God had given her to assist needy blacks in the South. She opened many schools. On one school her motto is inscribed above the entrance: "Enter to Learn." Above the exit are the words "Depart to Serve." She continually served others by educating them and providing them with medical supplies.

AN IMPOSSIBLE DREAM

Mrs. Bethune started with a seemingly impossible dream, but she worked until it became a reality. Have the children write a story about a dream they have to make their world a better place to live. Remind them to include steps they will have to take to make the dream come true.

GEORGE WASHINGTON CARVER

George Washington Carver was born in slavery. As a child he loved plants. When he became free, he obtained an education and dedicated his life to finding ways of helping the southern farmers. He showed them how to plant crops to enrich soil which had been depleted by overplanting of cotton. He found many uses for sweet potatoes and peanuts. He found that sweet potatoes could be used to make flour, cereals, glues, rubber and dyes. Altogether he found about 300 ways to use peanuts. Make a peanut butter pie.

PEANUT BUTTER PIE

1 large pkg. instant vanilla pudding
1½ cups milk
1¼ cups vanilla ice cream, softened
¾ cup peanut butter

Mix the pudding and the milk, then add ice cream and peanut butter. Blend well. Pour into a graham cracker pie crust and top with whipped cream. Freeze before serving.

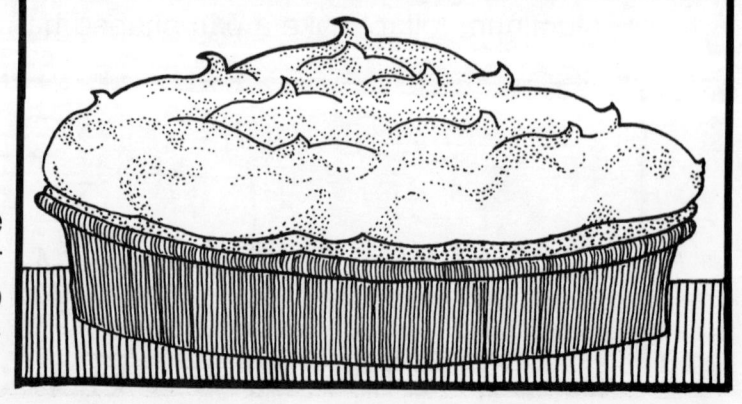

WOMEN WHO CHANGED THEIR WORLD
HARRIET BEECHER STOWE

Harriet Beecher Stowe wrote the book *Uncle Tom's Cabin* because she sympathized with the slaves and the hard lives which they led. She lived in Cincinnati on the Ohio River, and had seen many slaves crossing the river to escape from the slave state of Kentucky. She had also heard many stories of the wretched lives of slaves. The book aroused many people to fight against the evils of slavery.

Her brother, Henry Ward Beecher, was a very popular preacher who was also involved in the antislavery movement. Together they helped many slaves have better lives.

WRITE A STORY

Have the children write a story telling the reasons they think everyone should be free.

SUSAN B. ANTHONY

Susan B. Anthony was one of the early crusaders in the women's suffrage movement. She thought women should have the right to vote. Before her death, four western states had given women this right; but her goal was to pass a constitutional amendment which would give all women in the nation the right to vote. In 1920 the Nineteenth Amendment was adopted, thus giving women this right.

ELECTION DAY

Have an election to show the importance of the female vote. First have only the boys vote in an election for class officers. Then hold another election, this time giving the girls in the class the right to vote. Were the results different? How did the girls feel when they were not permitted to vote?

PIONEERS IN FLIGHT
WILBUR AND ORVILLE WRIGHT

Almost since the dawn of creation, man has envied the birds and has dreamed of flying gracefully through the air. Wilbur and Orville Wright were the first ones to attain this goal, by staying aloft for fifty-nine seconds in a power-driven airplane. Their historical flight at Kitty Hawk on December 17, 1903, marked the beginning of the age of flying. Success did not come easily, however. Prior to their successful flight, the brothers experimented with more than two hundred pairs of paper wings for their airplane.

A DESIGN CONTEST

Conduct a contest to determine which child can make and design a paper plane which stays in the air for the longest period of time, or which flies the longest distance.

AWARD CERTIFICATES

On the day of the contest, award as many certificates as possible. Be creative in determining categories: lowest-flying airplane, highest-flying plane, plane that flew the longest distance, best wing design, sleekest fuselage, most aerobatic etc.

AIRPLANE CONTEST

_____ designed an airplane which

_____

_____

on _____
       date

_____
       teacher

AMELIA EARHART

Amelia Earhart developed an excitement for flying when she was just a child. The driving ambition to pilot a plane helped her to discipline her life to reach her goal. She surpassed the dreams she had envisioned for herself by becoming the first woman to cross the Atlantic. Later, she became the first woman to cross the Atlantic alone. Her final goal was to fly around the world. She disappeared while flying over the Pacific Ocean on an ill-fated flight. She once quoted a line in a poem which stated, "Each time we make a choice, we pay with courage." She made some interesting choices in her life and courageously pursued each one.

FILE A FLIGHT PLAN

Pilots are required to file a flight plan before they depart for any destination. Have the children decide on a destination and then file a flight report.

FLIGHT PLAN RECORD

1. Type ___VFR ___IFR ___DVFR	2. Aircraft identification	3. Aircraft type Special equipment	4. True airspeed	5. Departure point
6. Departure time Proposed actual		7. Cruising altitude	9. Destination	
8. Route of flight				
10. Est. time en route	11. Remarks		12. Fuel on board Hours Minutes	
13. Alternate airports	14. Pilot's name, address, telephone number and aircraft home base			
15. Number aboard	16. Color of aircraft	17. Weather briefing	18. Stopover flight plan	
19. Time started	20. Pilot's initials			

ALEXANDER GRAHAM BELL

Alexander Graham Bell was the first scientist to succeed in transmitting human speech by wire. He had been a teacher of the deaf, and he wanted to devise a method so the deaf could hear sounds. As his experiments became more complicated, he asked an electrician, Thomas Watson, to join him. The pair worked long hours before they finally achieved success. The first words to come over the wire were, "Mr. Watson, come here. I want you." Countless words have since been transmitted.

NEW USES

New uses of the telephone are continually being made. One of the latest uses is a service called Dial-a-Prayer. Have the children compose a recording which could be used by other children when they Dial-a-Prayer.

LEE DE FOREST

Lee De Forest added platinum wire to one of Thomas Edison's incandescent light bulbs and devised a wireless method of transmitting voices. He invented a three-electrode vacuum tube, making radios possible. The development of radio was slow, because people did not think of it as a useful invention. For several years De Forest was the only broadcaster. When radio was finally developed, inventors used his ideas to take even greater steps into the electronic age of television and radar.

DEVELOP SOUND DEFFECTS

Radio broadcasts often used sound effects to make the circumstances on their programs seem real. Develop sound effects that could be used on radio programs. For example: For thunder, shake a sheet of metal. Footsteps could be made by placing shoes on the hands and walking them across the table. Wind can be made by blowing across the top of a pop bottle. By pulling a nail across a piece of glass, one can make the sound of a squeaking door. Rain can be made by pouring water from a garden watering can onto a sheet of metal. The faster the water is poured, the louder the rainfall becomes.

THOMAS ALVA EDISON

Thomas Edison once stated that genius is one percent inspiration and ninety-nine percent perspiration. He knew what he was talking about, because he tried many new ways of doing things. After 10,000 experiments with a storage battery, he said that he had not failed. He had just found 10,000 ways that would not work.

EDISON'S INVENTIONS

Although Edison had only three months of formal schooling, his brilliant inventions changed the lives of people all over the world. His greatest invention was the electric light bulb. He also invented a motion picture device, the phonograph, the mimeograph, and a stock ticker. He improved the inventions of other people. He wanted his inventions to be useful to ordinary people. He also wanted them to be easily repaired.

MAKE A COLLAGE

Make a collage of electrical devices which we have today. A department store catalog would be a good source of pictures.

SUCCESS AWARD

Select an area in which each child would like to succeed. Help him decide how to reach the goal. Present the Success Award when the goal has been attained.

SUCCESS AWARD

_____ was a success at _____

_____
teacher

"Happy is the man that findeth wisdom, and the man that getteth understanding."
Proverbs 3:13

TINKER WITH SOME NUTS AND BOLTS
HENRY FORD

When Henry Ford was very young, he showed an interest in mechanical things. He was always curious to know how things worked. One time he got himself into trouble when he took his brother's mechanical butterfly apart. The wheels and parts went everywhere. His brother thought he had ruined it; it looked like a hopeless pile of junk. However, Henry stayed up late that night and was able to put the butterfly back together as good as new. Anywhere there was a scrap of metal, wire, a few nails or screws, Henry would be busy tinkering to see what he could create.

METAL SCULPTURES

Ask the children to bring scraps of metal, nuts, bolts, screws and wire to school. Have them create a metal sculpture by arranging the items in an interesting way.

PRACTICE THE GOLDEN RULE

"Therefore all things whatsoever ye would that men should do to you, do ye even so to them . . . ."
Matthew 7:12

Henry Ford practiced the Golden Rule. He made a fortune on his cars, but he did not keep all of this money for himself. In 1936 he established the Ford Foundation. Its goal is to help people through grants for educational purposes. Millions of dollars have been distributed to organizations to help improve the quality of our lives.

Make a Golden Rule bookmark shaped like a car, to help remind children of their obligation.

ELIAS HOWE

Elias Howe, concerned over the hard work his wife had to endure to make clothes for their family, was inspired to invent a sewing machine. He used two needles in his invention, one with an eye at a point above the cloth, the other needle below the cloth, acting as a shuttle. The two threads combined to form a lockstitch. He was able to patent his machine in 1846. Several companies began to manufacture the machine. At first they would not pay Howe, but finally he was able to convince them that they were using his ideas. Then they paid him royalties for each machine they made. He became a rich man, and the country was richer because clothes could now be made faster and easier with machines.

A DEMONSTRATION

To demonstrate how much the machine has reduced sewing time, bring a serger to school and make a T-shirt for one of the children. If you are not a seamstress, enlist the help of a volunteer. A round-neck T-shirt can be made in about 15 minutes. Watching the machine sew and trim is an interesting experience for the children.

LEO HENDRIK BAEKELAND

After making a fortune from photography paper, Leo Hendrik Baekeland retired at 35 to his Yonkers, New York, estate. However, his creative mind was still active. He decided to use one of the buildings on his estate for a laboratory. He wanted to find a substitute for shellac. He experimented with substances used by earlier researchers, but he used them in a different way. Earlier chemists said that too much heat would make control of the substance impossible. Baekeland decided to add very high heat under pressure. The product he took from his oven one day was light and tough and would resist stains. He called his invention "bakelite." This is the product we now call plastic. The material revolutionized the manufacture of everything from automobiles to toys.

EVERY LETTER

See if the class can name one plastic item that begins with each letter of the alphabet.

GREAT AMERICANS
Words by Helen Kitchell Evans
Music by Frances Mann Benson

1. Our country is great Because we are free. We — have laws to protect our liberty. Daring men like Ben Franklin made America the land where we want to be.

2. Abigail Adams wrote letters of fame, A woman of greatness we now honor her name. Thomas Jefferson became president, — he vent — ing things even used to day.

3. Abe Lincoln worked hard, he studied at night, In his log home there was just dim candle light; when Lincoln became president, he did away with slav'ry, then all were free.

*America! America!
May God Thy Gold Refine*

SELECTING A PRESIDENT
ELECTION DAY

Election Day for national offices has been set as the first Tuesday after the first Monday in November. People go to their precincts, which are buildings in their neighborhoods, to vote for electors. The presidential candidate who receives most of the votes for the state receives all of the electoral votes. These electors then cast their ballots for the President.

SAMPLE ELECTION

Divide the class into two or three states and have a sample election. This will demonstrate how one candidate could get the most popular votes, but lose the election because he or she did not get the most electoral votes.

INAUGURATION DAY

On January 20 every four years, a President of the United States is sworn into office. He places his left hand on an open Bible and raises his right hand while he repeats the Presidential Oath. Immediately he is declared the President.

PRESIDENTIAL OATH

"I do solemnly swear (or affirm) that I will faithfully execute the Office of President of the United States, and will to the best of my ability, preserve, protect, and defend the Constitution of the United States."

INAUGURATION SPEECHES

The inaugural speeches include items which set the goals for the country during the next four years. They outline the President's hopes and dreams for the country. Have the children make an inaugural speech which would include their dreams for the country. What things would they want to see happen? What laws would they make? These could be placed in a booklet for everyone to read.

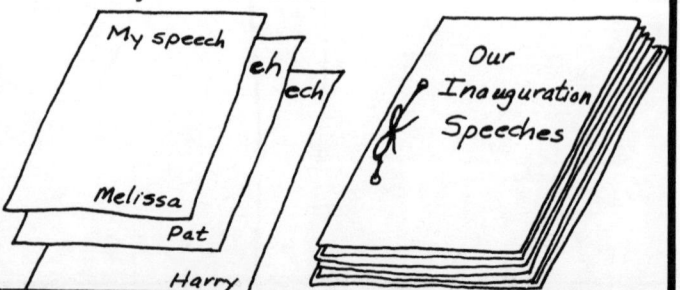

GEORGE WASHINGTON THE FIRST PRESIDENT

George Washington became the first President of the United States on April 30, 1789. He received 69 of the electoral votes. John Adams received 34, which made him Vice-President. Washington was inaugurated in New York City. The verse he chose to place his hand on while taking the Presidential oath was Psalm 127:1. Have the children learn this verse.

"First in war, first in peace, first in the hearts of his countrymen."

This phrase was a tribute which one of Washington's closest friends gave to him in summarizing his life of service to his country.

GEORGE WASHINGTON'S SCRIPTURE

"Except the Lord build the house, they labour in vain that build it: except the Lord keep the city, the watchman waketh but in vain.
Psalm 127:1

_____ has learned the verse on which George Washington placed his hand while taking the first Presidential Oath.

_____
Signature

A BUSY PRESIDENT

Building a new country seems like a monumental task for any man, and Washington was kept very busy. One of his first jobs as President was to draw up the Bill of Rights for the Constitution. Congress submitted twelve amendments for this Bill of Rights, ten of which were approved by the states. Washington also had to see that the government had funds to operate; so a tariff was imposed. Washington had to appoint secretaries for the different sections of government. The Postmaster General was appointed, along with the Secretary of War and the Secretary of the Treasury.

Have the children make a "List of Things to Do" which Washington might have made in starting our country.

THE ADAMSES MOVE IN

While George Washington had been responsible for the design of the President's house, it was not built until the end of John Adams' administration. John and Abigail Adams lived in it for only a few months. However, his prayer for the house now hangs over the fireplace in the State Dining Room. Franklin Delano Roosevelt had it placed there for all the visitors to see.

"I pray Heaven to bestow the best of blessing on this House and all that may hereafter inhabit it. May none but honest and wise men ever rule under this roof."

MAKE A POSTER

Make a poster of this prayer. It would be a good one to hang in any room.

I pray heaven to bestow the best of blessing on this House and all who may hereafter inhabit it. May none but honest and wise men ever rule under this roof.

FIRST LADY IN THE WHITE HOUSE

Abigail Adams was the daughter of a Congregational minister. She was a very practical lady who worked the farm while her husband John was serving his country. She tended dairy, fed the livestock, weeded the gardens and supervised the planting of the crops. When she moved into the White House, she used the unfinished East Room to hang her laundry. Even though she was practical, she still liked to have beauty around her.

QUILLING

One craft that was popular in Abigail Adams' time was quilling. Cut strips of paper 1/8" wide. Gold foil works well for this project. Roll the paper and form the rolls into interesting designs. They make a good border for a picture, or they can make up the entire picture.

THOMAS JEFFERSON AUTHOR OF THE DECLARATION OF INDEPENDENCE

When Thomas Jefferson was only 33, he wrote The Declaration of Independence. In this document he outlined the reasons why the colonies should break away from England and be a separate country. We celebrate the Fourth of July because it represents the time when the Declaration of Independence was approved by the lawmakers of the country and was signed by fifty-six people. This act started the move toward the Revolutionary War.

THOMAS JEFFERSON THE INVENTOR

Thomas Jefferson was a great statesman, but he was also a noted inventor. He devised many items which made his life easier. For his home he invented a clock that had cannonball weights; it also told the day of the week. He designed a revolving chair and a portable writing desk. He created a mechanical gadget for his closet that revolved and brought his clothes around to him. He also made automatic closing doors for his home.

There are many devices which would make our lives easier. Have the children think of some of their own. Make drawings of their inventions, and if possible make models.

THOMAS JEFFERSON BELIEVED IN RELIGIOUS FREEDOM

Thomas Jefferson believed that religious freedom was very important for the people of the new land. He introduced a bill into the Virginia Legislature that was designed to provide this freedom. When he wrote his own epitaph, he did not mention the fact that he was President; he wanted people to know that he was the one to help insure religious freedom.

"Here was buried Thomas Jefferson, author of the Declaration of Independence, of the statute of Virginia for religious freedom, and the father of the University of Virginia."

Have the children write epitaphs for Jefferson and other Presidents, pinpointing what they consider the important things in those administrations.

MILLARD FILLMORE

Millard Fillmore and his wife were teachers at one time. They were disappointed that the White House had no library, so Abigail Fillmore created one on the second floor. Congress appropriated $250 on March 3, 1851, to purchase books for the White House library.

BOOKS TO INCLUDE

Have the children select ten books they would like to include in the White House library for the children who will live there in future generations.

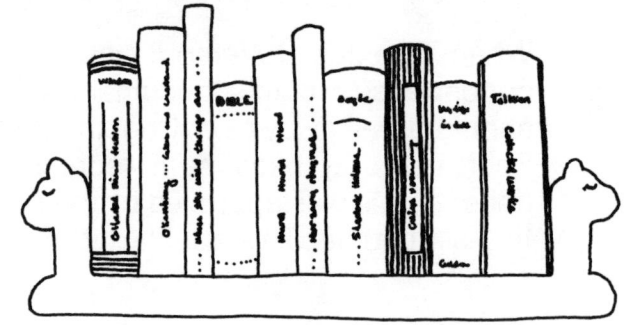

ABRAHAM LINCOLN

Abraham Lincoln's appearance was greatly changed by a letter he received from an 11-year-old girl. Grace Bedell told the President that he should let his whiskers grow because his face was so thin. Grace stated that all the ladies like whiskers, and they would ask their husbands to vote for Lincoln if he would grow a beard. At first, President Lincoln did not think he would follow her advice, but he later grew his famous beard.

COMPOSE A LETTER

Have children compose a letter to the President with a suggestion for either improving his appearance or suggesting a method of solving a national problem.

Use this address:
   (The President's name)
   The White House
   Washington, D.C. 20500

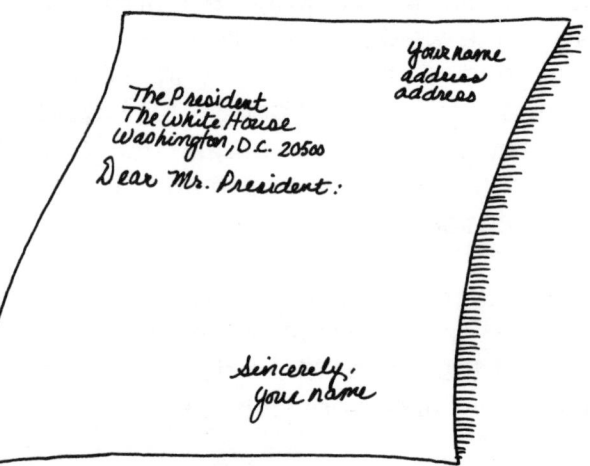

GROVER CLEVELAND

Grover Cleveland became President in 1885 and again in 1893. He got married while in the White House. He and his wife had five children. The candy bar Baby Ruth is named for President Cleveland's daughter.

A NEW RECIPE

Have the children make up a recipe for a new kind of candy bar. Include all kinds of delicious ingredients, and create an interesting shape for it. Name it after a family member of one of the past Presidents.

THEODORE ROOSEVELT

Theodore Roosevelt was known for his conservation ideals. Once when he was hunting he spared the life of a bear cub. Later, he was featured in a cartoon showing his concern for the little animal. A toy maker picked up on the idea and began making "teddy bears." Now they are a favorite of the young set.

TEDDY BEAR DAY

Have a Teddy Bear Day, when each child brings his teddy bear to share. For those who do not have a bear, make one from construction paper.

Make the body and head. Cut the legs separately. Attach these to the body with brad fasteners so they can move.

WILLIAM HOWARD TAFT

During the term of William Howard Taft, the income tax law came into existence. Now everyone must file an income tax statement with the Federal Government by April 15 every year.

Taft's wife loved beauty and wanted to make Washington, D.C., more colorful, so she started a campaign to plant cherry trees. The mayor of Tokyo gave her 3,000 trees. Today the Cherry Blossom Festival is enjoyed in Washington each year by thousands of visitors.

CHERRY TREE PROJECT

Make a cherry tree art project. With black crayon draw an outline of a tree. Cut small circles of pink construction paper, forming "cherries." Fold the paper loosely and glue the pieces onto the tree limbs.

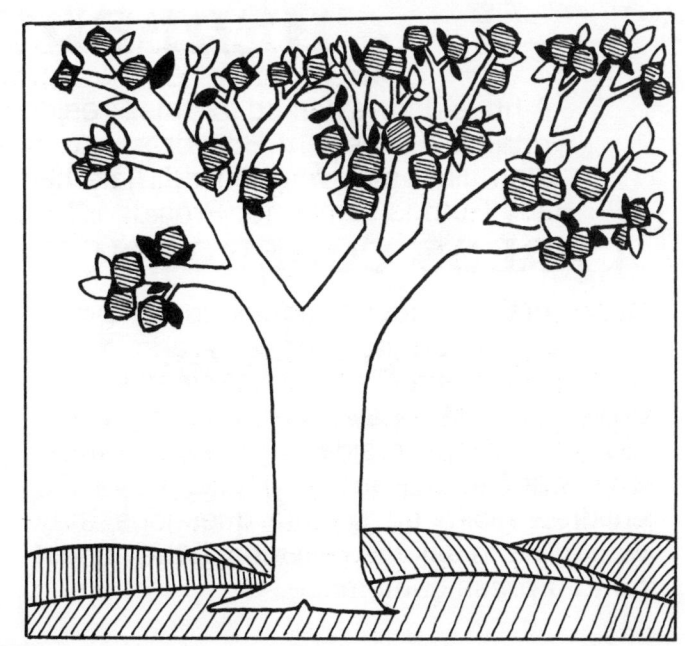

WOODROW WILSON

Woodrow Wilson had some very difficult times in his administration, since his tenure coincided with World War I. However, he had some happy times too. He was the first President to authorize the observance of Mother's Day, which he proclaimed an official holiday in 1914.

MOTHER'S DAY

Each family celebrates Mother's Day differently. Have the children plan unique ways in which they can honor their mothers on a daily basis.

CALVIN COOLIDGE

Calvin Coolidge was a man known for his thrifty ways and his reserved speech. When President Harding died, Coolidge was sworn into office by his father in a humble room in his Plymouth, Vermont, home. Because Coolidge talked very little and was a good listener, people nicknamed him "Silent Cal."

NICKNAMES

Other Presidents could have had nicknames based on some of their personal traits or actions during their administrations. See how many complimentary nicknames the children can find for the Presidents or their wives. For example: "Honest Abe" was a name given to President Lincoln. "The Star of the Show" might fit President Reagan, since he was once an actor. "Lemonade Lucy" was a first lady who would not serve alcohol in the White House. Can you identify her?

HERBERT HOOVER

A huge dam is named for this President. The Hoover Dam was one of his great projects. President Hoover's time in office coincided with the Great Depression. He had a very difficult time helping the people.

A PRESS CONFERENCE

Reporters were just beginning to use press conferences during Hoover's administration. This method of communication has grown so that today it is used almost exclusively when Presidents have something they want to say to the public. Have the children make up sample questions they would like to ask the President if they could go to a press conference.

FRANKLIN DELANO ROOSEVELT

Franklin Delano Roosevelt served the country as President longer than any other man. He led the United States for a little over twelve years. No other President will be able to remain in office for this length of time, because the Twenty-Second Amendment states that a President can serve only two terms.

President Roosevelt helped the country recover from the Great Depression and was also the country's leader during World War II. During the war many people were afraid. His famous words, "The only thing we have to fear is fear itself," helped the people through this crisis.

PRESIDENTS' SLOGANS

Other Presidents had slogans which were appropriate for their times. President Truman said, "The buck stops here."

President Kennedy's slogan was, "Ask not what your country can do for you. Ask what you can do for your country."

"This is the day which the Lord hath made; we will rejoice and be glad in it." Psalm 118:24

BIBLE VERSE TO HELP IN TIMES OF NEED

The Bible contains verses for every situation we encounter on this earth. Have the children find verses which will help them. Make bumper stickers they can use on their bicycles, using the verses they select.

"For the Lord God is a sun and a shield... no good thing will be withhold from them that walk uprightly." Psalm 84:11

"The fear of the Lord is the beginning of wisdom....," Psalm 111:10

DWIGHT EISENHOWER

Dwight Eisenhower took his oath of office on Tuesday, January 20, 1953. Before he gave his inaugural address, he prayed for God's blessing on his administration. He prayed:

"Almighty God, as we stand here at this moment, my future associates in the executive branch of government join me in beseeching that Thou will make full and complete our dedication to the service of the people in this throng, and their fellow citizens everywhere.

Give us, we pray, the power to discern clearly right from wrong, and allow all our words and actions to be governed thereby, and by the laws of this land. Especially we pray that our concern shall be for all the people, regardless of station, race, or calling.

May cooperation be permitted and be the mutual aim of those who, under the concepts of our Constitution, hold to differing political faiths; so that all may work for the good of our beloved country and Thy glory. Amen."

MAKE A BOOKMARK

Have the children select a portion of this prayer to write on a bookmark. Make the bookmarks from construction paper and then laminate them.

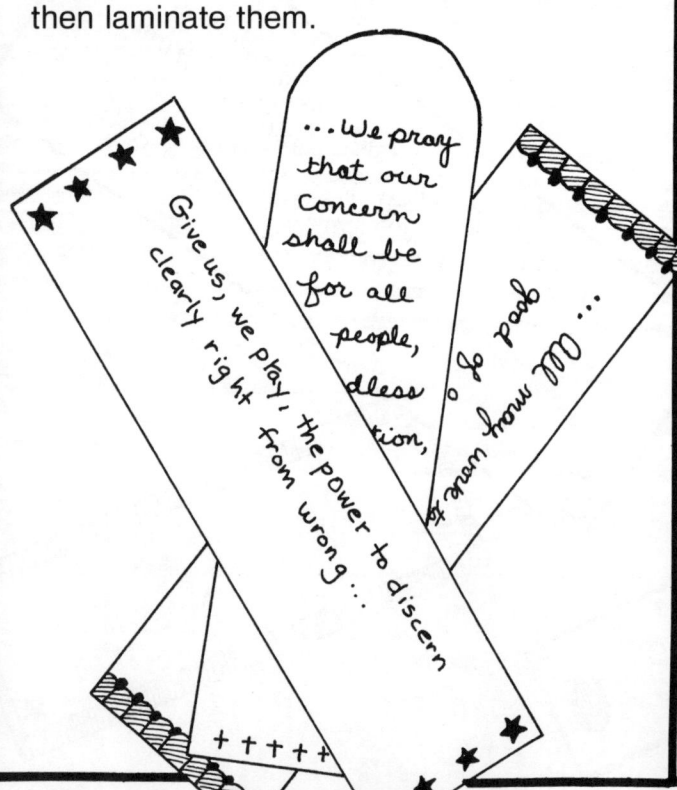

THE PRESIDENT'S HOBBY

Dwight Eisenhower liked to paint. However, his skills in drawing were very limited, so he had an artist draw pictures for him. Then he would paint them. This practice fostered a whole new line of merchandise. Manufacturers began making pictures that could be painted by number.

Duplicate the picture on the following page for the children to paint by number.

1 – Red
2 – light blue
3 – yellow
4 – dark blue
5 – dark green
6 – light green
7 – brown
8 – purple
9 – pink
10 – white

OUR PRESIDENTS
Words by Helen Kitchell Evans
Music by Frances Mann Benson

Great men have served us; Through years we've gained fame; Great men who served God and who treasured His name. And freedom for all was each President's goal; A freedom of worship for each living soul. Oh, God bless our country, Our country that is great; Let's keep Old Glory flying Over every state.

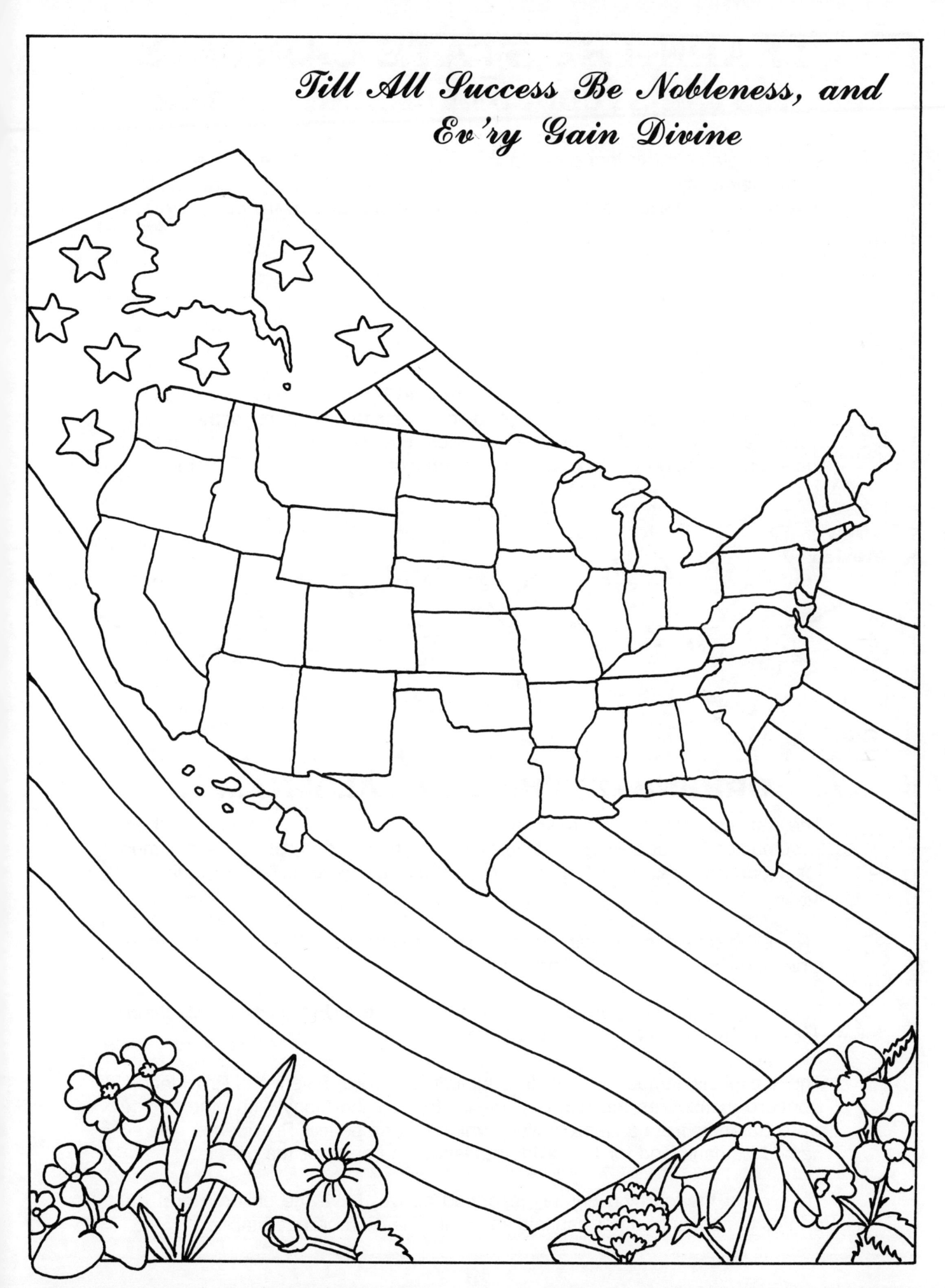

Till All Success Be Nobleness, and Ev'ry Gain Divine

LEARN THE STATE CAPITALS
A STAR-STUDDED LEARNING CENTER

Make a yellow star for each of the fifty states. Write the name of a state on each star and place in random order in the learning center. Make a blue star for each capital city, and write the capital's name on each one. Have the children match the capitals to the states by placing each blue star by the correct yellow star.

To make the center easier for younger children, it might be better to start with just a few states which are near your state and then branch out. A map of the states and capitals could also help them to learn faster. Remove the map as skill is developed.

For older children the center could be made more challenging by making another set or two of stars. A red set could contain the nickname of the state. A green set of stars could contain a fact about the state, a famous person from the state, an important product or a natural wonder found in that state.

ORIGINS OF THE CAPITALS' NAMES

The state capitals received their names in a variety of ways. About half of them were named for people who were important in their history. Some were named for geographic features around the city, and a few were named for their lofty ideas.

Two of the state capitals were named to honor Columbus. They are Columbus, Ohio and Columbia, South Carolina.

Four capitals were named to honor Presidents of the United States: Madison, Jackson, Jefferson City and Lincoln.

Those capitals named for lofty ideas include Concord, Salem and Providence. Concord symbolizes the peoples' desire to have harmony with others. The word **Salem** is from a Hebrew word which means peace. Providence was so named to thank God for His divine guidance and care for the people.

To expand the learning center described above, have the children find the origins of names of other capitals and write them on orange stars.

AMERICA'S BEAUTIFUL FLOWERS

All over America fragrant flowers cascade over the hillsides and valleys. Each state has selected one official flower to be its own. It is usually one that grows easily and abundantly in that state's climate. Sometimes the flower has special meaning for the people of the state. The forget-me-not of Alaska is the symbol of friendship.

SCHOOL CHILDREN SELECT NEW YORK'S FLOWER

New York was the first state to select an official flower. In 1891 the children in all of the schools were asked to choose a flower that they thought would be the best for their state. The rose was the most popular choice.

MAKE A STATELY BOUQUET

Using an encyclopedia, find the flowers of several states and make a "stately bouquet."

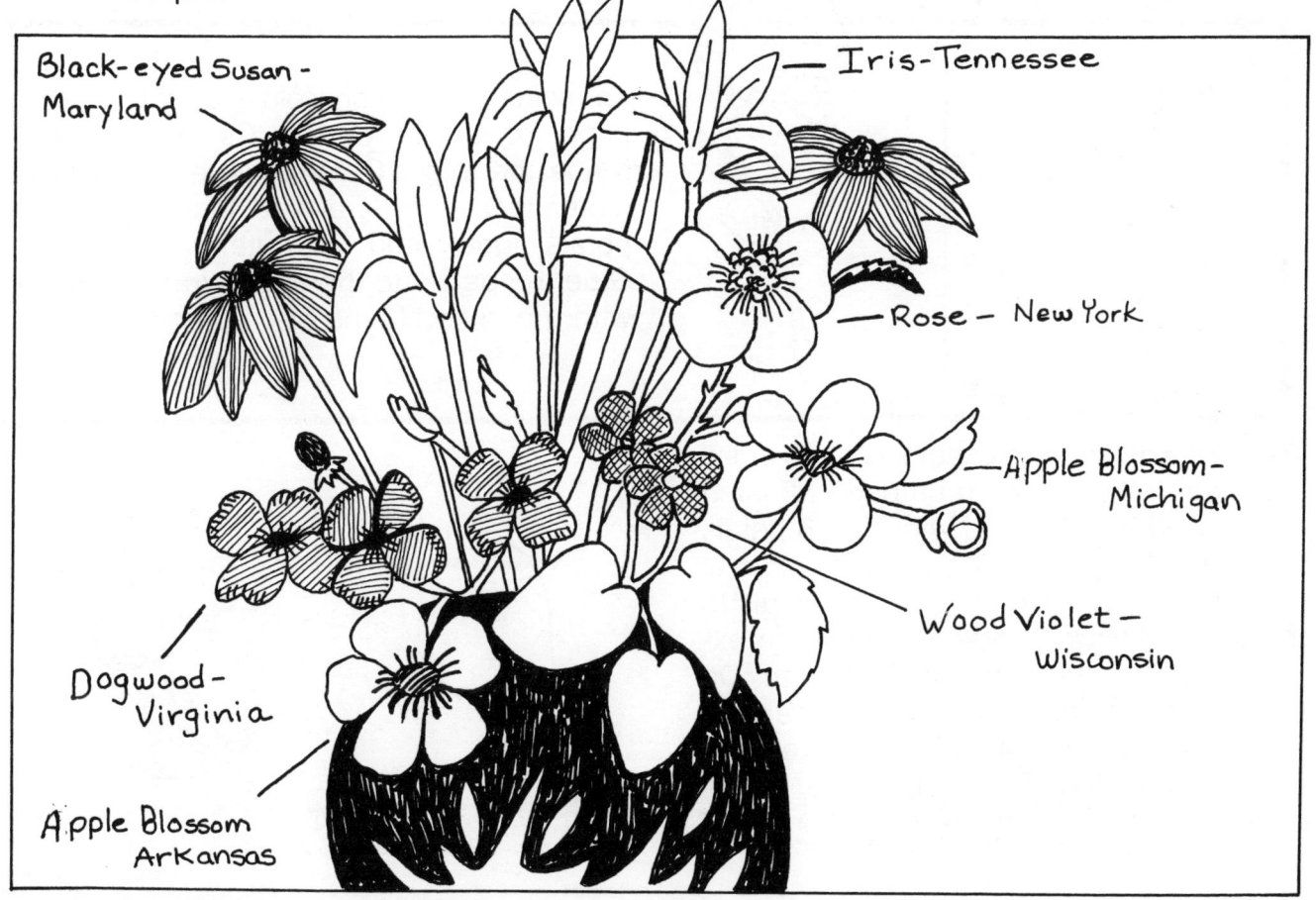

- Black-eyed Susan - Maryland
- Iris - Tennessee
- Rose - New York
- Apple Blossom - Michigan
- Wood Violet - Wisconsin
- Dogwood - Virginia
- Apple Blossom - Arkansas

STATELY FLOWERS

Several different kinds of flowers can be made from one set of directions. To make a rose, a geranium, an apple blossom or a poppy, cut out the shapes shown below. For each flower, first bend a long floral wire in two. Slip a small cotton ball over the folded portion and wrap it with crepe paper. Secure the crepe paper with wire along the bottom edge. Place the flower petal shapes around this basic center. Pull up the first ones to make a tight bud. Glue the petals to the wire at their base. Continue adding more petals until the flower is the desired fullness. Curl the outside edges by pulling them over a pencil. Add leaves. Cover the stem with green crepe paper.

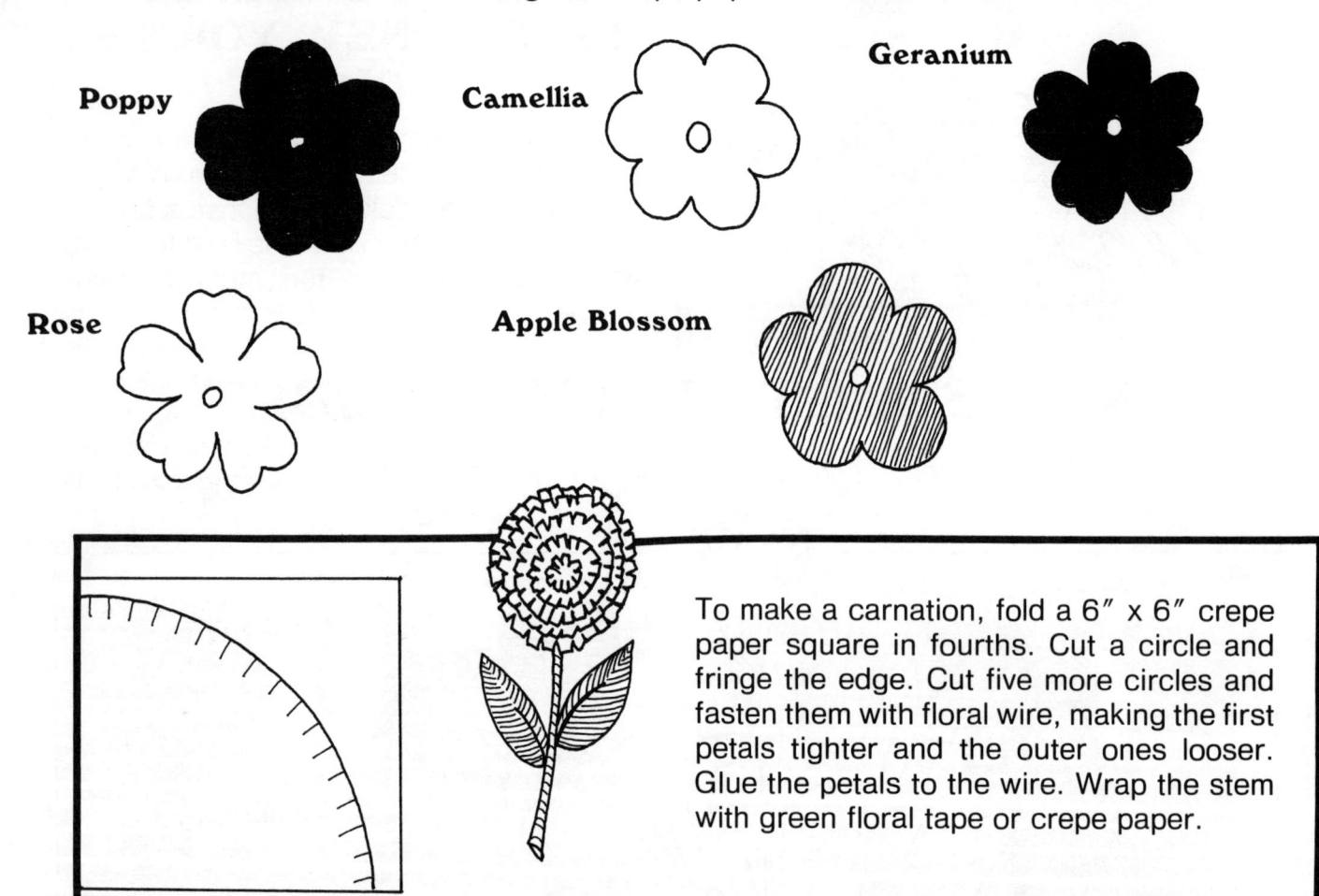

Poppy   Camellia   Geranium

Rose   Apple Blossom

To make a carnation, fold a 6" x 6" crepe paper square in fourths. Cut a circle and fringe the edge. Cut five more circles and fasten them with floral wire, making the first petals tighter and the outer ones looser. Glue the petals to the wire. Wrap the stem with green floral tape or crepe paper.

To make a dogwood blossom, cover 6 small split peas with brown crepe paper. Fasten them together with floral wire. Cut 8 petals for each flower. Sandwich a section of floral wire between two petals. Glue the petals to the wire, leaving a portion of the wire extending below the petals for the stem. Do the other three sets of petals the same way. Place the four sections together, wrapping all the wires together around the brown center with green crepe paper or floral tape.

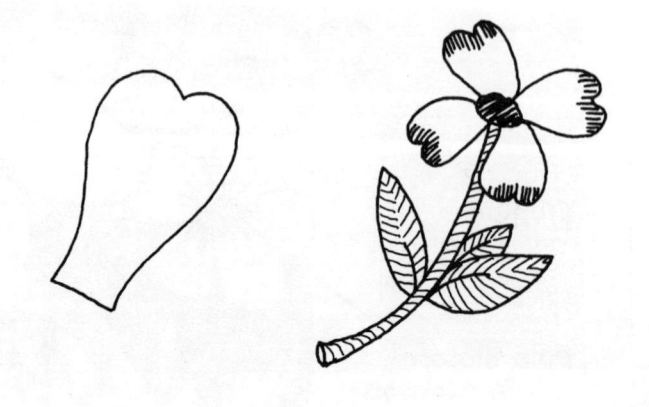

COLORFUL FLAGS REPRESENT THE STATES

State flags often have interesting stories behind them. None is more appealing to a child than that of the state of Alaska. A little Indian boy named Benny Benson, who attended a territorial school in Seward, entered a flag-making contest in 1926. He lived in a mission school because he had no parents. At night he loved looking out his window at the stars. He thought of Alaska as the North Star. Sometimes all of the stars in the heavens reminded Benny of the forget-me-nots he saw blooming in the fields. When he designed his flag, Benny wanted the stars to be as he had seen them at night, blanketing the beautiful Alaskan sky.

BENNY'S FLAG

In Benny's flag, gold stars formed the outline of the Big Dipper. The Big Dipper is also part of the Great Bear constellation, which symbolized the strength of the Alaskan people. The background represented the blue sky and the forget-me-nots which later became the state flower. The lone North Star represented Alaska's future statehood.

Read *Benny's Flag*, by Phyllis Krasilovsky.

DESIGN A NEW FLAG FOR YOUR STATE

Benny's classmates also entered the same contest. They had their own ideas about how the state flag should look. Study the present flag of your state. Redesign it, including items you think are important which the original maker overlooked or decided not to include. Tell what each item in the flag represents.

LEARN MY MOTTO

Each state has selected a motto to express its feelings about itself. Some refer to civil rights. Alabama declares, "We Dare Defend Our Rights." Kentucky asserts, "United We Stand, Divided We Fall." Texas wanted to extend southern hospitality by proclaiming, "Friendship."

Florida	"In God we trust." This is also the motto of the United States.
Arizona	"Ditat Deus," which means "God enriches."
Colorado	"Ni sine Numine," which means "Nothing without Providence."
Hawaii	"The life of the land is perpetuated in righteousness."
Ohio	"With God all things are possible."
South Dakota	"Under God the people rule."

Find out the motto for your state. Often material is available from the State House explaining the reason for this motto's selection. Write a letter requesting this information.

MAKE UP A MOTTO FOR YOUR SCHOOL

Have a contest in which each child composes a motto for the school. Choose the winner in an election.

Under God We Learn

Jesus Is Our Teacher

"Take fast hold of instruction . . . keep her; for she is thy life."

Proverbs 4:13

Have each child write a motto for his life. Consider the values he thinks are important. Also consider how he wants to look in the eyes of God and in the eyes of other people.

An acronym would be appropriate:
"Have
A
Pleasant
Personality
Yourself."

A portion of a song could provide a good motto: "I am a child of the King."

Scripture could be used for a motto:

"I can do all things through Christ which strengtheneth me." Philippians 4:13

Letters of the alphabet could be used:

"Always Be Considerate."

The child's personal motto may be made in the form of a banner so it could be hung in his room at home.

WHAT'S IN A NICKNAME?

Colorful stories are told of how some states acquired their nicknames. Some of them were selected as a result of a significant occurrence in their history. Oklahoma is one of these states. It is called The Sooner State, a name originated when some land in Oklahoma was first opened to settlers. People who wanted this land were to line up at the border and then go in and stake out their claims at the proper time. They were called Sooners because they went in before they were supposed to enter.

Some states' nicknames refer to vegetation growing there. Missisippi is called The Magnolia State, and Maine is The Pine Tree State.

Animals provide another source of nicknames. Michigan is The Wolverine State because trappers brought so many of the pelts of wolverines to the early fur-trading posts in the area. Minnesota is The Gopher State because so many of the creatures were found in its southern portion.

Sometimes a geographic location is used for the nickname. Massachusetts is called The Bay State because the Puritans settled around Massachusetts Bay. Rhode Island is called The Ocean State because of its position on the coast.

Some states have patriotic nicknames. Colorado is called The Centennial State because it joined the Union in 1876, when the United States was 100 years old. Many states have more than one nickname. Pennsylvania is called The Keystone State because it formed the center of the thirteen original colonies. It is also called The Quaker State to honor its founder, William Penn, who was a Quaker. Connecticut is known as The Constitution State. However, George Washington gave it another nickname. Because the state supplied large amounts of food, clothing and other staples to the army during the Revolutionary War, he called it The Provision State.

FIND OUT

Find out the nickname for your state. Usually there are other nicknames which might be equally appropriate. The particular one chosen was just one that seemed right at that time. Another nickname might be more meaningful now.

A NEW NAME

Select a new nickname for your state. It may be serious or humorous. However, each name should have some significance for the state. For example, Idaho is called The Gem State. It could also be called The Great Potato State, The Skier's Paradise, or The Lumberjack State.

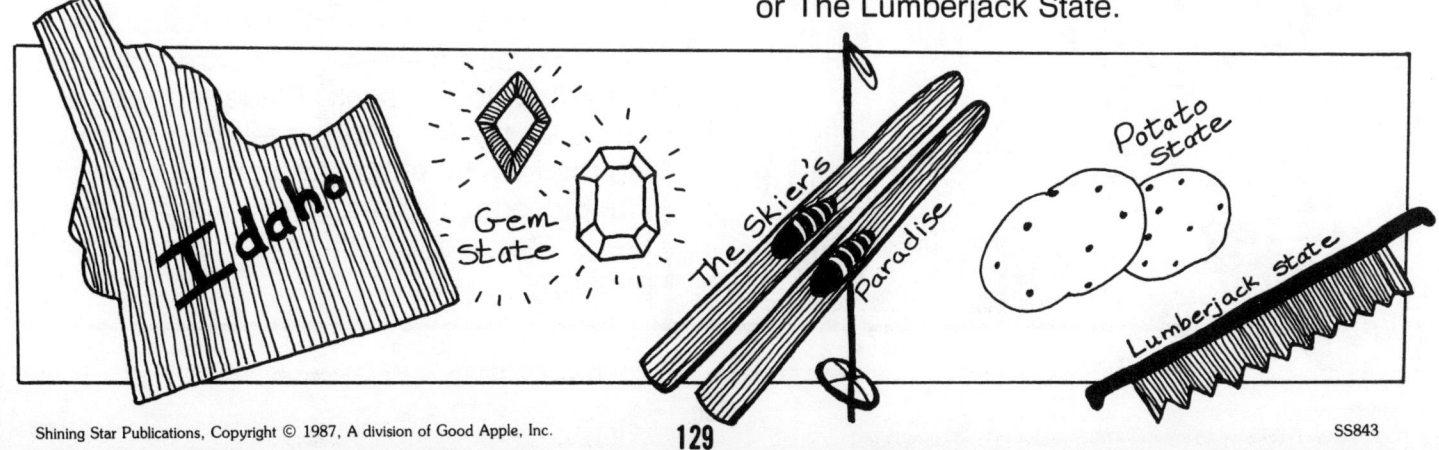

AMERICA'S BEAUTIFUL BIRDS

The beauty of America is enhanced by its wide variety of birds. Each state has adopted a favorite one. Connecticut, Michigan and Wisconsin have named the robin as theirs. There is an old English legend about how the robin got its red breast. While Christ was on His way to the cross, a robin carried a thorn from His crown in its beak, and a drop of blood fell from it. The blood spread over the breast and dyed it red.

Robins are considered friendly birds. They like to be around people. After a long winter, the sighting of a robin gives hope to northerners that spring is near.

YELLOWHAMMER

The state bird for Alabama is the yellowhammer. It is also one of the state's nicknames. During the Civil War a company of soldiers paraded in uniforms trimmed with bright pieces of yellow cloth. The people said the soldiers reminded them of the birds called yellowhammers, which have yellow patches under their wings. After that, the Alabama troops were called the Yellowhammers.

Other states have interesting bird tales. Find your state bird. If there is not already an interesting story connected with it, make up one.

MAKE A FINE FEATHERED FRIEND

Find a large picture of a state bird. Cover the picture with a piece of clear plastic wrap and color the bird with felt pens; you will not harm the original picture. Be careful not to move the plastic wrap. When finished with the coloring, remove the wrap from the original and lay aside. Tear a piece of aluminum foil about the size of the picture. Crumple it into a ball and then straighten it out. It should have a lot of creases. Place the foil over a piece of cardboard, and tape the edges to the back. Place the bird picture over the foil with the felt-pen side facing the foil. Tape the plastic wrap by bringing the edges to the back and securing them. Mount the picture on construction paper.

MAKE A CLASSROOM HERITAGE MAP

Many children in your class probably were born in another state. Make a large outline map of the United States, showing all the states, and hang it on a wall. On the map show where all the children were born. Have the students find out where their parents were born and mark those locations also. If there is still room to write, add the birthplaces of grandparents. See how many states are included in the classroom heritage tree.

To extend this activity, the children may make their own personal maps. They may record events that took place in the cities or states where they or their families visited or lived.

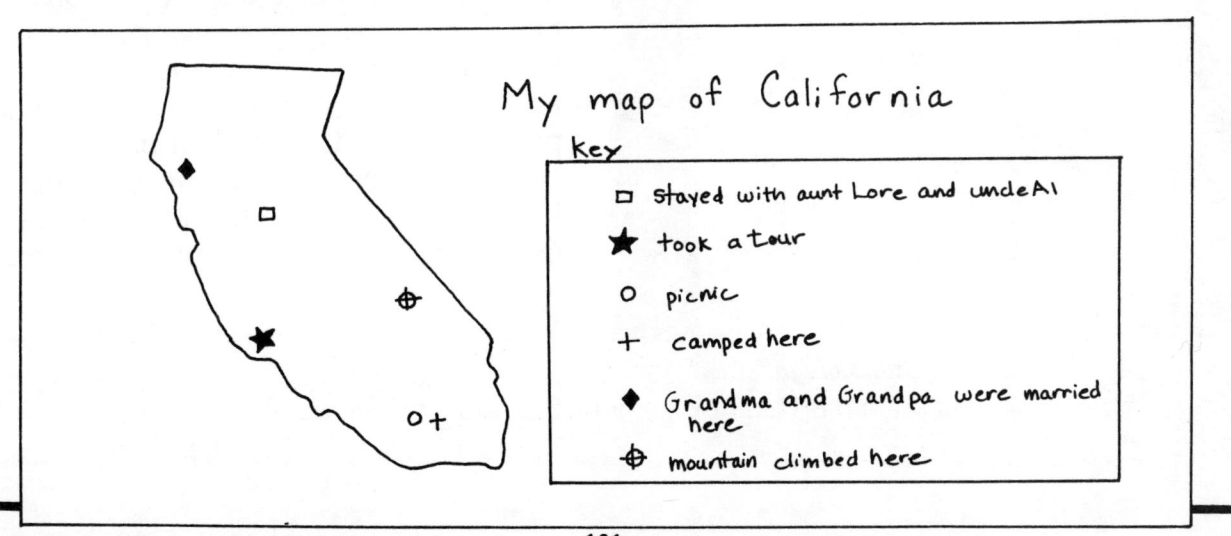

My map of California

Key

- □ stayed with aunt Lore and uncle Al
- ★ took a tour
- ○ picnic
- + camped here
- ◆ Grandma and Grandpa were married here
- ⊕ mountain climbed here

MAKE A TOURIST'S GUIDE FOR YOUR STATE

A CHILD'S VIEW OF THE STATE

The ordinary sights and sounds which surround us each day may be quite extraordinary to a visitor. Have the children make up a tour of your state, telling an outsider about special places of interest. Be sure to include annual events which occur in the state. Have each child describe a place or an event. They can give it a homey touch by discussing their topic with grandparents, whose recollections might be different from the child's present viewpoint. Organize the material into a geographic pattern so that a talking tour can be made around the state.

FOR EXAMPLE:
Arizona is rich with scenic beauty. The Grand Canyon is a spectacular sight. The state also has 15 national monuments, including Organ Pipe Cactus, Montezuma Castle and Sunset Crater. Special events include the sunrise service at the Grand Canyon on Easter morning, hot-air balloon races, and cactus shows.

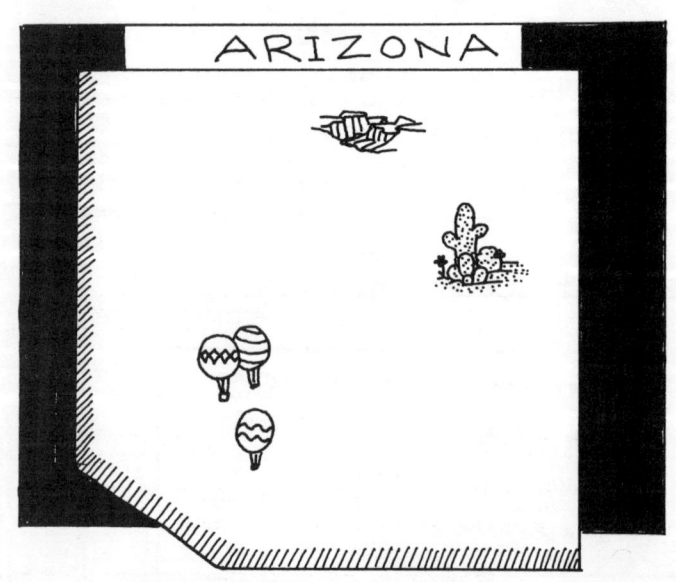

EVERYONE IS IMPORTANT

Every person who lives in your state is important, because it is the people who give a place shape and character. Interview senior citizens to find out as much as possible about how they shaped your state. Prepare questions for the children to ask the seniors about their occupations, hobbies, and their volunteer work. The importance of their home life and church affiliation should also be explored. To bring the project closer to the children, have them determine ways in which **they** are important in your state. What contributions are they making to the school, church and home?

"Even a child is known by his doings, whether his work be pure, and whether it be right."

Proverbs 20:11

STATES MAKE UP AMERICA
Words by Helen Kitchell Evans
Music by Frances Mann Benson

States come in all siz-es But ev-ery one is great.
They make up A-mer-i-ca Which we cel-e-brate.
Cel-e-brate our free-dom, Our great lib-er-ty.
God bless A-mer-i-ca, The land for you and me.
Yes, God bless A-mer-i-ca, The land of the free.
Let us stand with pride and sa-lute the flag we see.

CELEBRATE AMERICA WITH US

You are cordially invited to attend our patriotic day "Celebrate America" at _____
                                                                            time

on _____
              date

at _____
              place

Presented by
_____

CELEBRATE AMERICA

—Cast of Characters—

Uncle Sam
Pilgrim children:
   Giles Hopkins
   Remember Allerton
   Barth Allerton
Rebecca—a pioneer girl
Meriwether Lewis
Jack—a stagecoach traveler

Four contemporary children:
   Jason
   Bill
   Jeni
   Lisa
Daniel Boone
William Clark

Setting: A city park. Four children are sitting on park benches watching a chorus perform. A patriotic backdrop is behind the children.

CHORUS: *("America, the Beautiful." During the song, slides of American landscapes should be shown on a screen beside or above the chorus.)*

JASON: We have a wonderful country!

JENI: The best in the whole world!

(Enter Uncle Sam)

UNCLE SAM: Yes, children, we do have an outstanding country.

BILL: *(jumping up and speaking in a surprised voice)* Uncle Sam, where did you come from? I didn't know there was a **real** Uncle Sam.

UNCLE SAM: Oh yes, Bill. I've been around since our country began. Some people made me famous during the War of 1812, but I have always been in the hearts of Americans. I have watched our country grow from a small handful of people to millions.

LISA:	Were you here when the Pilgrims landed?
UNCLE SAM:	I was here when the Pilgrims landed and when the first satellites were launched into space.
JASON:	Did you see the first American flight, when Alan Shephard went into space?
UNCLE SAM:	I saw it all, and I'll be here to see the day when school children will take field trips into space. I heard the chorus learning a song about their trip to space.
CHORUS:	*("Our Rocket Ship," page 14)*
JASON:	It must have been exciting to see so many happenings in our country. Tell us about the Pilgrims.
UNCLE SAM:	They were an ambitious group of people. They had to work hard to prepare for their first winter. Sometimes the Pilgrims are called Founding Fathers. That is a good name for them; but did you know that there were also many children on the Mayflower? But they can tell their story better than I can. Here they come now.
	(Enter Pilgrim children)
UNCLE SAM:	Hello, Giles, Barth and Remember. My friends would like to know about the early days, when you lived. What can you tell them?
GILES:	When we arrived there were very few people living in the country. We had to learn survival skills quickly. The Indians helped us grow food and gave us many tips on how to live in our new country.
LISA:	In my history book I read about your trip on the Mayflower. Were you afraid during the storm at sea?
REMEMBER:	That **was** a frightening time. During the storm the great beam on the Mayflower broke. The women and children were all rushed below deck.
	The men and boys struggled to fix the beam. It took many hours to repair. The men were exhausted when the job was finished, but they were happy, because they knew they had saved the ship and the lives of all the people on board.
JENI:	How did you feel when you finally arrived in your new land?
BARTH:	We were thankful that we had made a safe trip. However, we were even more grateful to God that He had given us a place where we could worship as we pleased. In our country we were punished for serving God in our own way. We all offered a prayer of thanksgiving to God.
BILL:	How did you manage to get ready for winter?
GILES:	Our days were filled from dawn until dusk building shelters and gathering supplies for winter. Everyone had to work—even little children.

JENI:	Did you ever have time to play?
REMEMBER:	There wasn't much time for games. Besides, our parents thought children should be taught to work. Some believed that playing was sinful.
UNCLE SAM:	The early settlers had very little time to play. Later, parents and children often worked together to make homemade toys. *(Enter Rebecca, wearing a bright bonnet and colorful dress. She should be carrying a rag doll.)*
UNCLE SAM:	Rebecca can tell you about her playtime.
REBECCA:	I loved to play with my dolls. Mother made me the prettiest cornhusk doll! I named her Molly. My sister, Anna, had a floppy rag doll. We carried our dolls everywhere.
BILL:	What did the boys play?
REBECCA:	The boys loved to roll hoops down the road. Sometimes they had races to see who could roll the hoop the farthest before it dropped on its side.
JENI:	It sounds like you had fun just like we do.
CHORUS:	*("Pilgrims," page 74)* *(Exit Pilgrim children and Rebecca)*
UNCLE SAM:	After the Pilgrims arrived, many other groups of people came to the new land seeking freedom. It wasn't long before the coastland was crowded. People wanted to move west.
JASON:	It was hard to move west in those days, because the mountains were in the way. The people did not know how to get through them.
UNCLE SAM:	That's right. The mountains seemed impassable. That is why men like Daniel Boone were so important to our young country. They blazed wide trails through the mountains so the pioneers could travel on them. *(Enter Daniel Boone)*
UNCLE SAM:	Daniel, you have some mighty interesting tales for the young ones here. Tell them how you happened to become a pioneer trailblazer.
DANIEL:	Adventure was in my blood. I loved danger and excitement. When I was just a boy, I often visited a friendly Indian tribe that lived near our farm. They taught me all I know about Indian ways. While I was helping my dad at home, I would dream about the day when I could leave home and explore great new lands.
BILL:	When did you first get your chance to explore?
DANIEL:	When I was about twenty years old, a man told me about a rich hunting land to the west. I could hardly wait to be on my way. Some friends joined me. It didn't take us long to discover a narrow Indian pathway through the mountains.

LISA:	Weren't you sometimes afraid when you met hostile Indians?
DANIEL:	I was afraid many times, but I used the tricks I had learned from my childhood Indian friends to outsmart my enemies.
UNCLE SAM:	Daniel Boone was very clever, not only when he met Indians, but also in making trails for the pioneers. He widened that first Indian trail he found. People later called it "The Wilderness Road." Through this passage the pioneers could get to Kentucky and all points west. Thank you, Daniel. America appreciates your courage and daring.

(Exit Daniel Boone)

JASON:	Other men helped to explore our Far West. Meriwether Lewis and William Clark were asked to find a waterway to the western boundary of the country.

(Enter Lewis and Clark)

BILL:	Did you find the waterway, men?
LEWIS:	We found that no waterway existed. But we did make it to the western boundary. What a trip! I will never forget it. Many times I thought we were doomed. We survived one disaster after another. Sometimes hostile Indians tried to steal our precious equipment. The weather was cold and rainy. The high mountains seemed almost too steep to climb.
JENI:	It's a miracle you were able to live to tell your story. But I remember one bright spot in the journey. That was the day you met Sacagawea. Tell us about her.
CLARK:	Sacagawea was a gift from God. She was an Indian girl who agreed to travel with us. Her knowledge of the Indian people and the western lands helped us to survive in almost impossible situations. Without her expert help the expedition probably would have failed.
UNCLE SAM:	Thanks to Lewis, Clark and Sacagawea, the West was opened for new settlers.

(Exit Lewis and Clark)

UNCLE SAM:	So many people were moving to the West that there was a need for public transportation. They didn't have cars and buses, but stagecoach lines became available for businessmen and travelers of all sorts.

(Enter Jack, wearing several layers of clothing with pockets bulging with supplies)

UNCLE SAM:	Jack often took the stagecoach to visit his clients in the West. Tell my friends about traveling on the stagecoaches.
JACK:	Riding the stagecoach was a mighty hair-raising affair. Indians and robbers knew the routes. An ambush could be around the next bend in the road. The drivers had to be alert all the time.

JASON:	That does sound exciting! But tell me, Jack, why are you wearing so many clothes? And why are your pockets bulging?
JACK:	Oh, the stagecoach rider had to be very creative to pack all of the supplies necessary for the trip. The baggage limit was 25 pounds. The passengers had to provide for all of their needs during the trip. *(Pulls cloth-wrapped sandwich and apple from one of his pockets)* This is for my lunch on the first day. *(Pulls washcloth from another pocket)* This will help me wash the day's dirt from my face. And all these clothes—well, I wear them so I would not have to pack them. I will need them when I get out West.
UNCLE SAM:	Thanks, Jack. Before you leave, listen to the song the children learned about the West.
CHORUS:	*("A Part of History," page 88)*
	(Jack leaves as song ends)
UNCLE SAM:	The West called to people in all parts of the country. They came on the stagecoaches. Others came on the prairie schooners. Some rode horses; some even walked to the West. As they moved west, they saw some spectacular sights.
LISA:	I wonder how they felt when they looked at the huge Grand Canyon?
JASON:	The Rocky Mountains must have been an overwhelming sight!
BILL:	I would like to have been with the group that was the first to see the mighty Mississippi River.
JENI:	God created many beautiful sights in our country for us to enjoy.
CHORUS:	*("Long Ago," page 32)*
UNCLE SAM:	It wasn't long before thousands of people had seen those beautiful sights. The news traveled back to the old countries. People from many lands began to come to America. We became known as the "melting pot." Do you know the land of your ancestors?
LISA:	I don't know about my ancestors, but my friend Rosa's parents came from Spain. I love to celebrate Christmas with her. It is their custom to go from house to house pretending they are Mary and Joseph looking for a place to stay in Bethlehem.
BILL:	Yes, and after all of their friends have been visited, everyone has a big pinata party.
UNCLE SAM:	Many countries of the world have shared with us their traditions, customs and foods.
JASON:	I love April Fool's Day; that was started in France.
JENI:	All the girls like French perfumes.

BILL:	The Italians showed us how to make their pizza and pasta dishes.
LISA:	They also shared their beautiful music.
JASON:	I like the fascinating puzzles the Chinese developed for everyone to enjoy. I could spend hours working on tangrams.
JENI:	The Japanese came to our shores in later years. They added their Haiku to our poetry. Isn't it wonderful to have so many cultures in our land?
CHORUS:	("God of Everyone," page 62)
UNCLE SAM:	The leaders of many lands allowed their people to come to America. These people brought their many talents and great minds to help us solve some of our perplexing problems. They also used their creativity to develop inventions to make our lives more interesting. Let's play a game to see if you can tell me how these people helped America. Are you ready?
CHILDREN:	We're ready.
UNCLE SAM:	Thomas Jefferson.
LISA:	He wrote the Declaration of Independence.
UNCLE SAM:	The Wright Brothers.
BILL:	They made and flew the first airplane.
UNCLE SAM:	Amelia Earhart.
LISA:	She was the first woman to fly solo across the Atlantic Ocean.
UNCLE SAM:	Henry Ford.
JASON:	He put America on wheels when he made the Model T Ford.
UNCLE SAM:	Harriet Tubman.
JENI:	She helped free many blacks by working in the Underground Railroad.
UNCLE SAM:	You are too good. You know all of these famous Americans. Our young country needed people from all walks of life. It needed great inventors, social workers, political leaders, good teachers, and wise statesmen to make laws to protect our freedoms.
CHORUS:	("Great Americans," page 110)
UNCLE SAM:	One of our first great leaders was George Washington.
LISA:	Yes, he was our first President. My teacher told us that he was a good leader. He wanted to establish a strong country. When he was sworn in as President, he selected a very special Bible verse on which to build our country.
JASON:	I remember that verse. The whole class learned it. Psalm 127:1. "Except the Lord build the house, they labour in vain that build it: except the Lord keep the city, the watchman waketh but in vain."

UNCLE SAM:	I'm glad your teacher taught you that verse. It gave a good start to our country. Many Presidents have followed George Washington. Do you remember the first President to live in the White House?
JENI:	That was John Adams. His wife, Abigail, used the East Room as a laundry room. She hung her clothes in there to dry.
UNCLE SAM:	Which President was an inventor?
BILL:	That was Thomas Jefferson. His house was filled with his inventions. He made a portable writing desk. He designed a revolving chair. The doors in his house closed automatically. He also made a gadget that made it easier to get his clothes from the closet.
UNCLE SAM:	Yes, our past Presidents were inventive and great thinkers. They led our country in times of peace and in times of war. They worked hard to keep our freedoms.
CHORUS:	*("Our Presidents," page 122)*
JASON:	When George Washington was President, our country was very small. How did we get so many states?
UNCLE SAM:	As the explorers pushed west, new lands were added to our country. These territories were then divided into states.
JENI:	The country doubled in size when the Louisiana Purchase was made. Many states were made from this huge portion of land.
LISA:	Later Texas and the West Coast were added to the country.
BILL:	Hawaii and Alaska were latecomers to our country.
CHORUS:	*("States Make Up America," page 133)*
JASON:	Have you visited all of the fifty states, Uncle Sam?
UNCLE SAM:	Oh, many times. What a sight it is walking through the cornfields of Iowa or through the Oregon wheat fields.
LISA:	God has blessed our land with rich soil to grow many crops. We have lots of apples and peaches in my state.
BILL:	Potatoes and alfalfa are grown where I live.
CHORUS:	*("America's Beauty," page 24)*
UNCLE SAM:	As I travel from state to state, I see many symbols of the freedoms that unite our country. In New York the Statue of Liberty reminds me how fortunate we are to have these freedoms.
LISA:	Our flag is a symbol of our liberty too. You can see it flying in all fifty states.
JASON:	In Pennsylvania you can see the Liberty Bell. It reminds us of our freedom too.
UNCLE SAM:	Yes, and even I am a symbol of freedom. But behind all of these symbols are the documents which established our freedom.

JASON:	Do you mean The Declaration of Independence?
BILL:	And the Constitution of the United States?
LISA:	And The Bill of Rights that was added to the Constitution?
JENI:	And the Emancipation Proclamation that helped to free the slaves?
UNCLE SAM:	It looks like you know about many of the documents which make our country strong. The country's motto is also very important in keeping our country great. We need to remember it—"In God We Trust."
CHORUS:	("Great Democracy," page 94)
UNCLE SAM:	Children, we have looked at our country from its simple beginnings to the present **united** fifty states. Join me in singing about this great country. *(Children stand with Uncle Sam and sing)*
CHORUS:	("America, the Beautiful")

TIPS FOR "CELEBRATE AMERICA"
SCENERY

Decorate the wall behind the characters with a large American flag. This can be made by taping red and white strips of crepe paper to the wall. A blue field should be added to the corner.

The children should be sitting in a park. To give this atmosphere, set some potted plants around the area.

COSTUMES

Directions for making a hat for Uncle Sam are found on page 43. Striped crepe paper pants and shirt complete his outfit.

The Pilgrim girl should wear a dark sunbonnet and a long dark dress. The Pilgrim boys should wear dark pants. Rubber bands worn around the knees allow the pants to be pulled up and bloused out to look like Pilgrim breeches. Knee socks should be worn.

Rebecca should wear a bright colored sunbonnet and a colorful long dress.

Ideas for Daniel Boone's costume can be found on page 99. Lewis and Clark should be dressed in similar costumes.

PATRIOTIC AMERICAN

Certificate of Award is presented to

_____

for excellent performance as

_____

in

CELEBRATE AMERICA

_____
Date

_____
Signature